AIRCRAFT
ARCHIVE

FAMOUS RACING AND AEROBATIC PLANES

CTM

Argus Books
Argus House
Boundary Way
Hemel Hempstead
Herts HP2 7ST
England

First published by Argus Books 1989

© In this Collection Argus Books 1989

ISBN 0 85242 999 1

Designed by Little Oak Studios
Phototypesetting by Typesetters (Birmingham) Ltd
Printed and bound in Great Britain by
William Clowes Ltd, Beccles and London

Cover photo: Two of the world's most
famous racing and aerobatic aircraft:
the scarlet 'Grosvenor House' DH88
Comet Racer and the chrome yellow
Pitts S-1S flown by Mary Gaffeney,
Women's World Champion, are typical
of the selection which follow in the
pages of this volume.

AIRCRAFT ARCHIVE

FAMOUS RACING AND AEROBATIC PLANES

C TM

Contents

A DETAILED COLLECTION OF ORIGINAL SCALE AIRCRAFT DRAWINGS

Introduction

All the previous nine volumes in this series of *Aircraft Archives* have been concerned with production machines or, at least, those which were intended for manufacture in quantity. Now we venture into the world of experimental types, expressly designed for very special purposes and capable of remarkable performance in terms of either manoeuvrability or speed – in some cases a combination of both characteristics.

It has always been an area of aeronautics where the glamour of achievements in the full glare of publicity is intermixed with frustrations, disasters and spectacular incidents. The aircraft are colourful and shapely and in all cases they reflect great individuality. Largely for these reasons, they have always been popular subjects for modelling. Indeed, many are so suited in their proportions that they are much like 'blown-up' models themselves.

Air racing and stunt or aerobatic displays have been a feature of entertainment programmes wherever the aeroplane has developed since the early days of flight. Sponsorships and prize offers have stimulated the daredevil instincts of engineers and pilots who have tempted providence with adventurous changes in their efforts to outperform the opposition in a highly competitive field. Not all have succeeded, but those who have done so have attained a level of fame with a single aircraft which has rivalled the public awareness of a whole production line.

There have been hundreds, even thousands of these 'one-offs' over the years and it is inevitable that the selection of just twenty-one for this volume will not satisfy the keen reader and merely whets the appetite for more. But this collection represents an international range, from the Government-supported to the homebuilt, from the low-budget creation to the product of unlimited expenditure in the name of the national flag-waving and prestige.

The perils attached to radical experiment with powerful engines in lightweight airframes was never more evident in those great years during the 1930s – often called the 'Golden Age' of air racing in the United States – when annual events based in Cleveland produced regular batches of minimum shapes attached to maximum-size engines. So here we have the stubby Gee Bee RI to compare with the sleek Folkerts Jupiter, the Chester Jeep and the intruding French Caudron which temporarily upset the pattern by actually winning its races.

Then there are the international seaplane racers, created for the Schneider Trophy by Supermarine, Curtiss, Gloster and Macchi-Castoldi – each of them an advance in technology which acclerated engineering development at a rapid pace, breaking records year by year. Which brings us to the Mew Gull and De Havilland 88 Comet, two unforgettable

◄ Veteran Tiger Moth 'CDC leads a pair of Tiger Club Stampe SV-4s in tied-together formation at RAF Biggin Hill Air Fair; the similarity of the two types is obvious. The SV-4, a developed version designed in Belgium but used mostly in France, is one of the drawings in this volume; the De Havilland 82A Tiger Moth appeared in *Aircraft Archive* 'Classics of World War Two'.

◄ A A P 'Pat' Lloyd doing what he likes best – obtaining his measured-from-life drawings of aerobatic, experimental and similar aircraft. A talented illustrator, he is here at work on the brand-new 1989 Extra 300 two-seat aerobatic aircraft, for future publication. Pat's technique involves hundreds of dimensions, taken by tape measure, coupled with innumerable photographs in order to produce something which the original manufacturers cannot offer. His classics are the series of Pitts drawings, now a world standard for detail research.

designs (happily still well preserved), each of which achieved both racing success and long-distance records to make them all-time favourites with enthusiasts everywhere.

In more recent years, enthusiasm for racing has been tempered by sheer cost, and even though regulation through a formula for standards of engine size, areas and cockpits has been imposed, these efforts to make air racing both safer and affordable have not produced the numbers anticipated. Nevertheless, Tom Cassutt's Formula One racer and its British rival the Rollason Beta have upheld the traditions, and for those with unlimited resources the annual meeting at Reno in Nevada is an exciting outlet for overpowered conversions of piston-engined fighters.

The aerobatic arena is a little different, as the drawing selection indicates. Before the arrival of purpose-designed individual machines, the private enthusiast was best served by trainers which were, in the first instance, created for fully aerobatic performance, such as the celebrated Tiger Moth, Stearman PT-17 or Bücker Jungmeister. These machines have been featured in the companion volume *Classics of World War Two*. Here we add three other 'Classics' of their kind. Russia's Yak 18 standard trainer was re-engined and modified to become a formidable competitor, and so too was the Bücker Jungmann from Germany and the French Stampe SVA-4 – all two-seat machines which have excelled in their time and still remain in favour with clubmen.

Specialist aircraft heading into the 1990s are tending to become stereotyped, but this cannot be said of Jim Bede's odd BD-8 with its independent elevators for rapid roll and extraordinary short coupling. Though a 'one-off' of little competitive value, it illustrates the range of diversity and, with the Acrostar which has coupled flaps and elevators as on a control-line aerobatic model, it typifies the innovative period of the 1960s and 1970s. But there are none more famous nor successful than Curtis Pitts' little biplane which started life as a medium-powered homebuilt and has since swept the world in many variations. The S-1 remains for many the pick of the bunch. So to those production machines from the USSR and Czechoslovakia, the Sukhoi Su-26 and the Z1lin 50L. Each an aristocrat with refinements only made possible with State-aided facilities, they form a benchmark which any new creations will have to match, or prove superior to.

Our draughtsmen for this volume are as specialised as their subject matter. Their work is already internationally renowned through publication in *Aeromodeller* and *Scale Models International* for the detailed study they have made of their subjects and the accuracy with which they have drawn some very elusive aeroplanes. Few drawings are available for these experimental types. The tape measure, hours of serious study and an uncanny ability to interpret photos correctly are linked with a sound engineering background and a professional career in design draughtmanship in each instance.

We are indebted to the skills of Pat Lloyd and Harry Robinson for what follows in this volume. It is thanks to them that collector, student and modeller now have access to precise detail of these fascinating machines.

A specialist on racing aircraft, with a penchant for Caudrons and Gee-Bee's, Harry Woodman has established inimitable standards for draughtmanship and in-depth study of high performance aircraft

▼

De Havilland DH88 Comet

Country of origin: Great Britain.
Type: Two-seat racing aircraft
Powerplant: Two De Havilland Gipsy VIR engines each rated at 215–220hp.
Dimensions: Wing span 44ft 0in *13.41m;*
length 30ft 0in *9.14m;* height 12ft 4¼in *3.78m; wing area 188.5 sq ft 17.51m².*
Weights: Empty 3002lb *1361kg;* maximum 5500lb *2494kg.*
Performance: Maximum speed 237mph
382kph; service ceiling 19,000ft *5790m;* range 2925 miles *4710km.*
First flight: 1934.

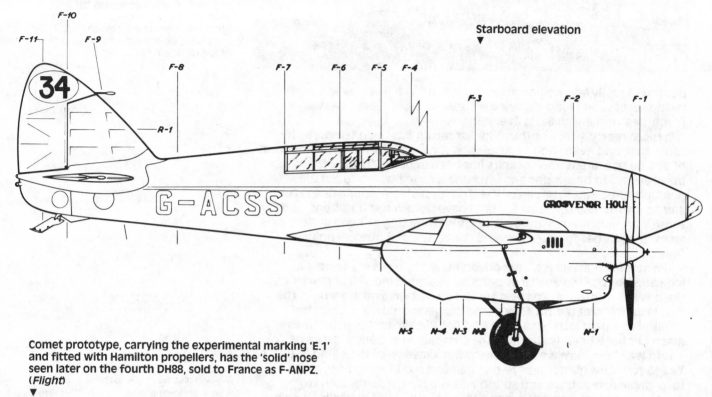

Starboard elevation ▼

Comet prototype, carrying the experimental marking 'E.1' and fitted with Hamilton propellers, has the 'solid' nose seen later on the fourth DH88, sold to France as F-ANPZ. (*Flight*)
▼

Scale

```
0   1   2   3   4   5   6   7   8 ft
|HHHHHH|---|---|---|---|---|---|---|
0               1               2 m
```

▲
The eventual England to Australia race winner 'Grosvenor House' in its famous red and white livery prior to the start at RAF Mildenhall. (*Flight*)

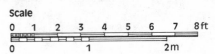

DIAGONAL RIB (SEE ELEVATIONS)
HORIZONTAL RIB
FIN RIBS WITH LIGHTENING HOLES
SPAR INTEGRAL WITH FORMER

R-1   ONE & A HALF TIMES GIVEN SCALE
PLYWOOD COVERING

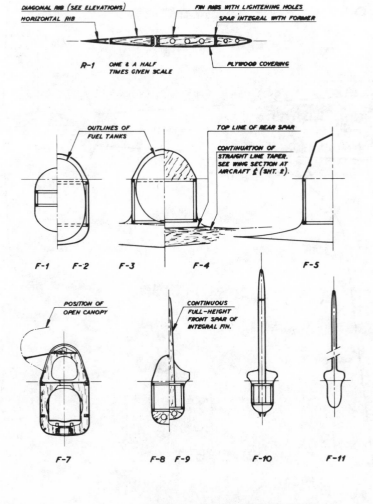

OUTLINES OF FUEL TANKS
TOP LINE OF REAR SPAR
CONTINUATION OF STRAIGHT LINE TAPER. SEE WING SECTION AT AIRCRAFT ℄ (SHT. 2).

F-1   F-2   F-3   F-4   F-5

POSITION OF OPEN CANOPY
CONTINUOUS FULL-HEIGHT FRONT SPAR OF INTEGRAL FIN.

F-7   F-8 F-9   F-10   F-11

SECT. F-6 IS SHOWN WITH COCKPIT VIEWS ON SHT. 2.
HORIZONTAL DATUM IS SHOWN IN LINE WITH HIGHEST POINT OF UPPER LONGERONS.

▲
Fuselage cross-sections

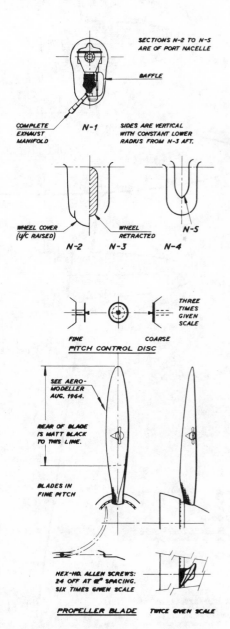

SECTIONS N-2 TO N-5 ARE OF PORT NACELLE
BAFFLE
COMPLETE EXHAUST MANIFOLD   N-1   SIDES ARE VERTICAL WITH CONSTANT LOWER RADIUS FROM N-3 AFT.

WHEEL COVER (U/C RAISED)   WHEEL RETRACTED   N-5
N-2   N-3   N-4

THREE TIMES GIVEN SCALE
FINE   COARSE
PITCH CONTROL DISC

SEE AERO-MODELLER AUG. 1964.
REAR OF BLADE IS MATT BLACK TO THIS LINE.
BLADES IN FINE PITCH

HEX-HD. ALLEN SCREWS: 24 OFF AT 8° SPACING. SIX TIMES GIVEN SCALE

PROPELLER BLADE   TWICE GIVEN SCALE

Scrap views ▶
Propeller details

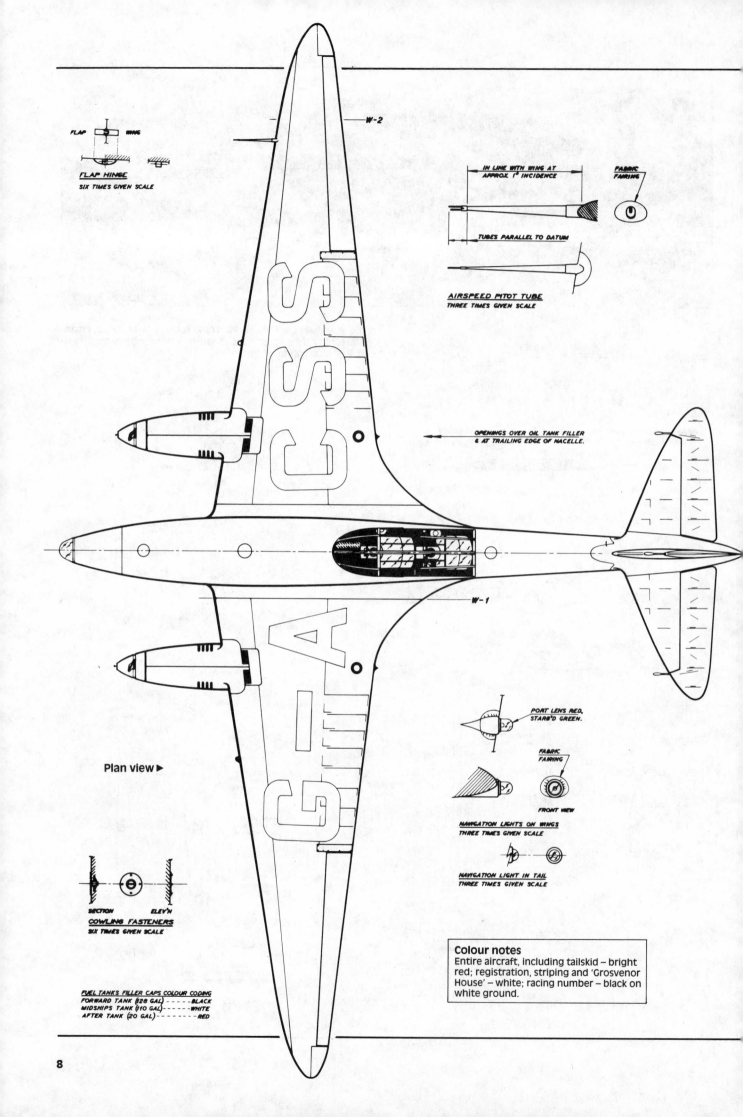

FLAP HINGE
SIX TIMES GIVEN SCALE

FLAP   WING

IN LINE WITH WING AT
APPROX. 1° INCIDENCE

FABRIC
FAIRING

TUBES PARALLEL TO DATUM

AIRSPEED PITOT TUBE
THREE TIMES GIVEN SCALE

W-2

CSSS

OPENINGS OVER OIL TANK FILLER
& AT TRAILING EDGE OF NACELLE.

W-1

G-A

Plan view ▶

PORT LENS RED,
STARB'D GREEN.

FABRIC
FAIRING

FRONT VIEW

NAVIGATION LIGHTS ON WINGS
THREE TIMES GIVEN SCALE

NAVIGATION LIGHT IN TAIL
THREE TIMES GIVEN SCALE

SECTION   ELEV'N
COWLING FASTENERS
SIX TIMES GIVEN SCALE

Colour notes
Entire aircraft, including tailskid – bright
red; registration, striping and 'Grosvenor
House' – white; racing number – black on
white ground.

FUEL TANKS FILLER CAPS COLOUR CODING
FORWARD TANK (128 GAL) - - - - - - BLACK
MIDSHIPS TANK (110 GAL) - - - - - - WHITE
AFTER TANK (20 GAL) - - - - - - - RED

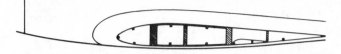

SECTION W-1 WITH BOTTOM LINE OF FUSELAGE & OUTLINE OF WING FILLET

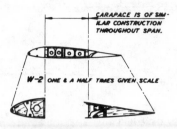

CARAPACE IS OF SIM-
ILAR CONSTRUCTION
THROUGHOUT SPAN.

W-2 ONE & A HALF TIMES GIVEN SCALE

NOSE & AILERON DETAILS
THREE TIMES GIVEN SCALE

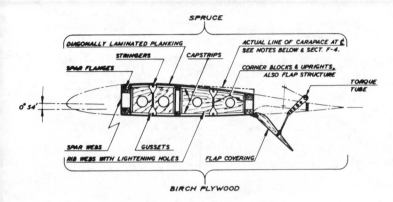

SPRUCE

DIAGONALLY LAMINATED PLANKING

STRINGERS

CAPSTRIPS

SPAR FLANGES

ACTUAL LINE OF CARAPACE AT ℄
SEE NOTES BELOW & SECT. F-4.

CORNER BLOCKS & UPRIGHTS,
ALSO FLAP STRUCTURE

TORQUE
TUBE

0° 54'

SPAR WEBS

GUSSETS

RIB WEBS WITH LIGHTENING HOLES

FLAP COVERING

BIRCH PLYWOOD

WING SECTION AT AIRCRAFT CENTRELINE, SHOWN
AS TRUE & COMPLETE RAF 34 AEROFOIL.
UPPER SURFACE BETWEEN NACELLES & AFT OF 40% CHORD IS IN FACT
MODIFIED TO SUIT REFLEX CURVE OF FILLETS AS SHOWN THUS — — — — —
NOTE SHAPE OF REAR SPAR SHOWN IN SECT. F-4, ALSO SECTS. F-5 &
W-1 ON SHEET 1.
STRUCTURAL DETAILS ARE TYPICAL.
STRAIGHT-LINE TAPER OF WING EXTENDS FROM CENTRELINE TO TIP
SECT. W-2 AT LEFT.
ACTUATING LEVERS OF AIR BRAKES ARE LOCATED 18" EACH SIDE OF
AIRCRAFT CENTRELINE.
SECTION IS ONE & A HALF TIMES GIVEN SCALE.

▲ Wing sections

RAF 34 AEROFOIL.	ALL VALUES ARE PERCENTAGES OF CHORD													
STAT'N	1·25	2·5	5	7·5	10	15	20	30	40	50	60	70	80	90	95
UPPER	1·97	2·83	4·11	5·05	5·82	6·98	7·72	8·33	8·08	7·22	5·83	4·31	2·70	1·26	0·64
LOWER	1·63	2·14	2·81	3·23	3·53	3·91	4·16	4·33	4·33	4·11	3·69	3·09	2·30	1·34	0·76

Mildenhall line-up, with 'Black Magic' in foreground,
Bernard Rubin's dark green and white 'SR No 19 and
Jaqueline Cochran's Granville 'QED' which retired at
Bucharest.
▼

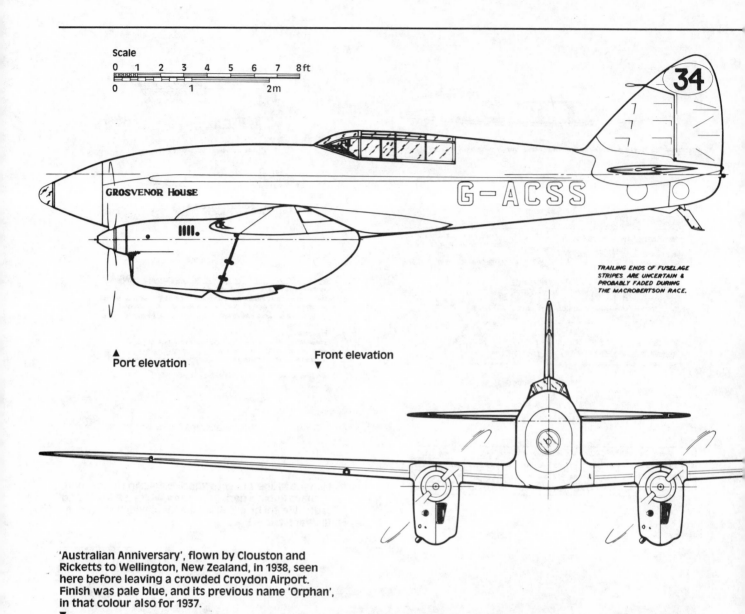

Scale

0 1 2 3 4 5 6 7 8 ft

0 ____ 1 ____ 2 m

34

GROSVENOR HOUSE

G-ACSS

TRAILING ENDS OF FUSELAGE
STRIPES ARE UNCERTAIN &
PROBABLY FADED DURING
THE MACROBERTSON RACE.

▲ Port elevation

Front elevation ▼

'Australian Anniversary', flown by Clouston and
Ricketts to Wellington, New Zealand, in 1938, seen
here before leaving a crowded Croydon Airport.
Finish was pale blue, and its previous name 'Orphan',
in that colour also for 1937.
▼

▲ The green Comet, flown by Owen Cathcart-Jones and Ken Waller for its owner Bernard Rubin and later sold as F-ANPY. (*Flight*)

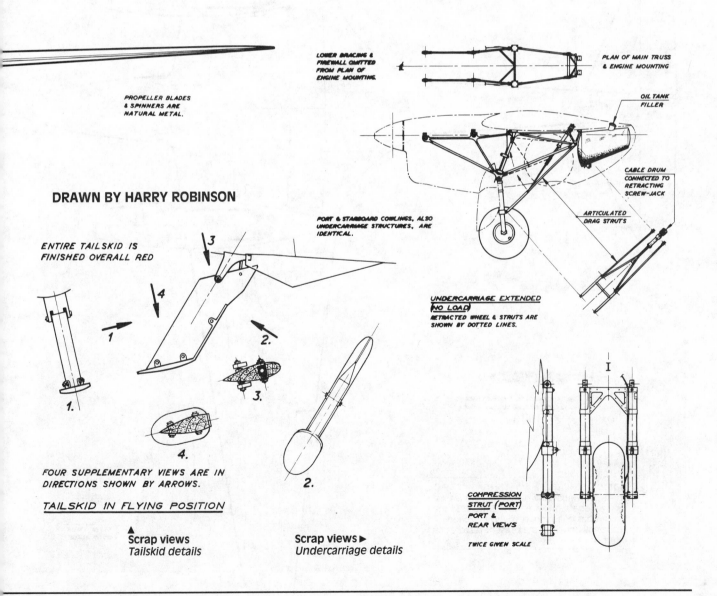

PROPELLER BLADES & SPINNERS ARE NATURAL METAL.

DRAWN BY HARRY ROBINSON

LOWER BRACING & FIREWALL OMITTED FROM PLAN OF ENGINE MOUNTING.

PLAN OF MAIN TRUSS & ENGINE MOUNTING

OIL TANK FILLER

CABLE DRUM CONNECTED TO RETRACTING SCREW-JACK

ARTICULATED DRAG STRUTS

PORT & STARBOARD COWLINGS, ALSO UNDERCARRIAGE STRUCTURES, ARE IDENTICAL.

ENTIRE TAILSKID IS FINISHED OVERALL RED

UNDERCARRIAGE EXTENDED (NO LOAD)
RETRACTED WHEEL & STRUTS ARE SHOWN BY DOTTED LINES.

1.
2.
3.
4.

FOUR SUPPLEMENTARY VIEWS ARE IN DIRECTIONS SHOWN BY ARROWS.

TAILSKID IN FLYING POSITION

2.

COMPRESSION STRUT (PORT)
PORT & REAR VIEWS

TWICE GIVEN SCALE

▲ **Scrap views**
Tailskid details

Scrap views ▶
Undercarriage details

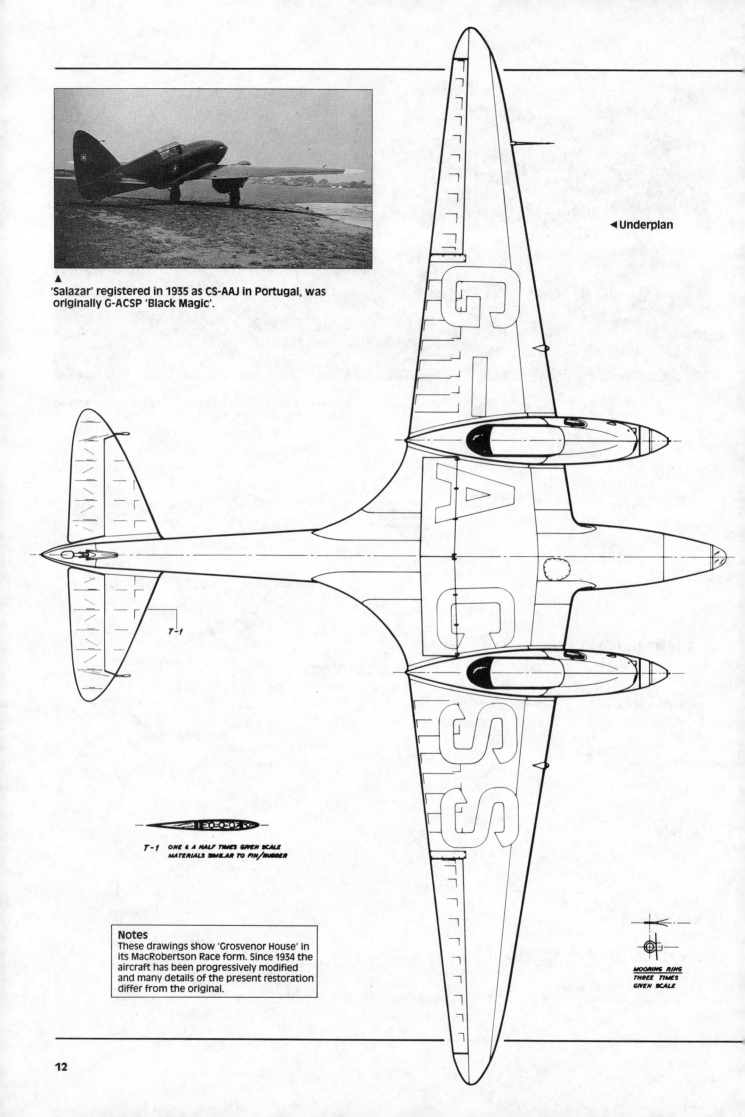

◄ Underplan

'Salazar' registered in 1935 as CS-AAJ in Portugal, was
originally G-ACSP 'Black Magic'.

T-1

T-1 ONE & A HALF TIMES GIVEN SCALE
MATERIALS SIMILAR TO FIN/RUDDER

MOORING RING
THREE TIMES
GIVEN SCALE

Notes
These drawings show 'Grosvenor House' in
its MacRobertson Race form. Since 1934 the
aircraft has been progressively modified
and many details of the present restoration
differ from the original.

Finished in RAF aluminium as K5084, G-ACSS appeared at the 1936 Hendon Air Display, later to revert to the civilian register before its eventual restoration to original state as today. (*Flight*)

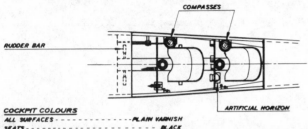

COMPASSES

RUDDER BAR

ARTIFICIAL HORIZON

COCKPIT COLOURS
ALL SURFACES - - - - - - - - - - - - - PLAIN VARNISH
SEATS - - - - - - - - - - - - - - - - - - - BLACK
THROTTLES, CONTROL LEVERS
& UNDERCARRIAGE WHEEL - - - - NATURAL ALLOY
KNOBS & LEVER TOPS - - - - - - BLACK VULCANITE
TOP DECKING FROM
WINDSCREEN TO FRONT PANEL - - - - MATT BLACK

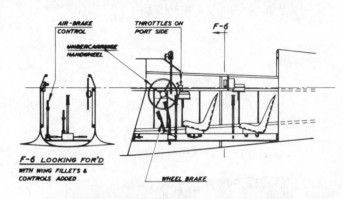

AIR-BRAKE CONTROL

THROTTLES ON PORT SIDE

F-6

UNDERCARRIAGE HANDWHEEL

F-6 LOOKING FOR'D
WITH WING FILLETS &
CONTROLS ADDED

WHEEL BRAKE

◄◄
Scrap views
Cockpit details

1989 Hatfield Open Day condition, when crosswinds precluded a flying demo, reinforcing the view that this precious vintage aircraft and its costly restoration demand the utmost respect. (R G Moulton)
▼

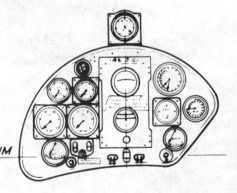

ATUM

FRONT INSTRUMENT PANEL

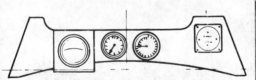

REAR INSTRUMENT PANEL

INSTRUMENTS ON MAIN FRONT PANEL ARE
NOT SHOWN IN COCKPIT VIEWS AT RIGHT.

PANEL COLOURS
FRONT PANEL - - - - - - - MATT BLACK
REAR PANEL - - - - VARNISHED TIMBER
INSTRUMENTS - - - BLACK BODIES, DIALS,
          WHITE MARKINGS.

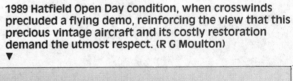

Gloster VI

Country of origin: Great Britain.
Type: Single-seat racing seaplane.
Powerplant: One Napier Lion VIID 12-cylinder engine rated at 1320hp.

Dimensions: Wing span 26ft 0in *7.92m*; length 27ft 0in *8.23m*.
Weights: Loaded about 3700lb *1678kg*.
Performance: Maximum speed

351.3mph *565.6kph*.
First flight: 25 August 1929.

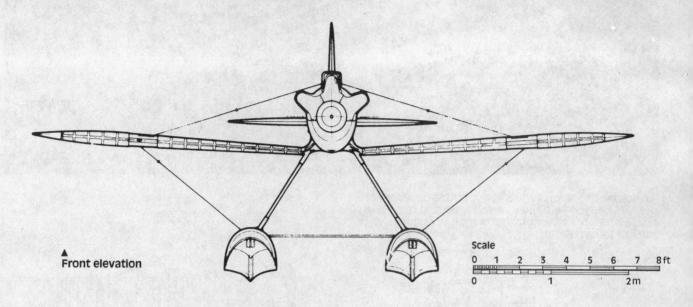

▲ Front elevation

Scale

| 0 | 1 | 2 | 3 | 4 | 5 | 6 | 7 | 8 ft |

| 0 | | 1 | | 2 m |

Surely the most elegant of all Schneider Racers, the Gloster VI used surface radiators on the fuselage which did not mar the shape. Elevator control was to a patented system. (*Flight*)

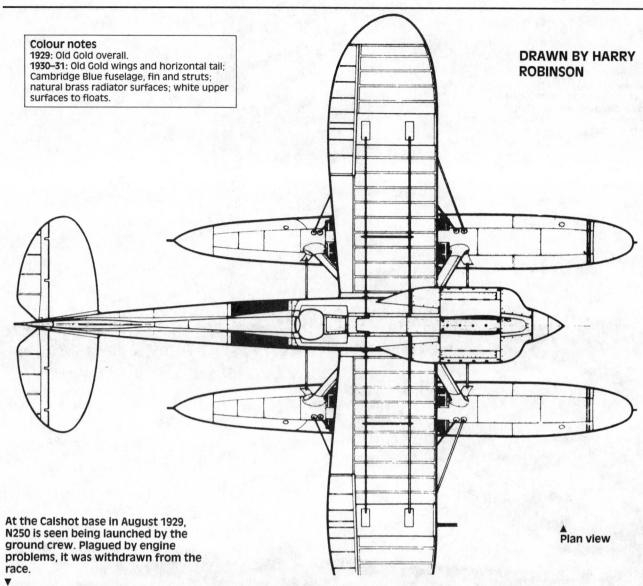

DRAWN BY HARRY ROBINSON

▲
Plan view

At the Calshot base in August 1929, N250 is seen being launched by the ground crew. Plagued by engine problems, it was withdrawn from the race.
▼

The twelve-cylinder three-bank engine was rated at
1,320hp for short periods but cut-outs in turns and after
take-off raised problems for pilots D'Arcy Grieg and
Orlebar. (*Flight*)

Scale

0 1 2 3 4 5 6 7 8 ft

0 1 2 m

F.1

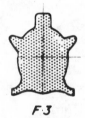

F.2

F.3

F.4

F.5

F.6

F.7

Fuselage cross-sections ▲

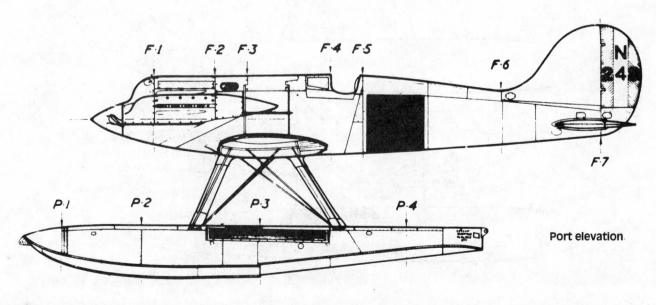

Port elevation

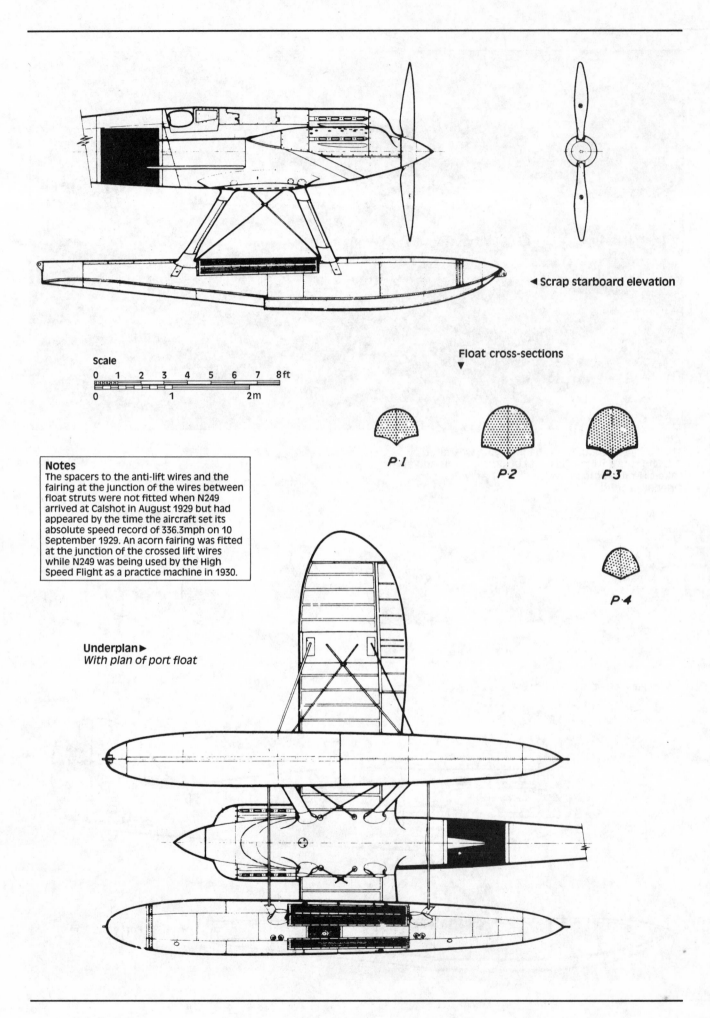

◄ Scrap starboard elevation

Float cross-sections
▼

P·1 P·2 P·3

P·4

Scale

0 1 2 3 4 5 6 7 8 ft

0   1   2 m

Notes
The spacers to the anti-lift wires and the
fairing at the junction of the wires between
float struts were not fitted when N249
arrived at Calshot in August 1929 but had
appeared by the time the aircraft set its
absolute speed record of 336.3mph on 10
September 1929. An acorn fairing was fitted
at the junction of the crossed lift wires
while N249 was being used by the High
Speed Flight as a practice machine in 1930.

Underplan►
With plan of port float

Percival Mew Gull E3H

Country of origin: Great Britain.
Type: Single-seat racing aircraft.
Powerplant: One De Havilland Gipsy VI Series II engine rated at 205hp.

Dimensions: Wing span 22ft 9in *6.93m*; length 20ft 3in *6.17m*; wing area 75 sq ft *6.97m²*.
Weights: Empty 1642lb *745kg*; loaded

2125lb *964kg*.
Performance: Maximum speed 265mph *427kph*.
First flight: 1937.

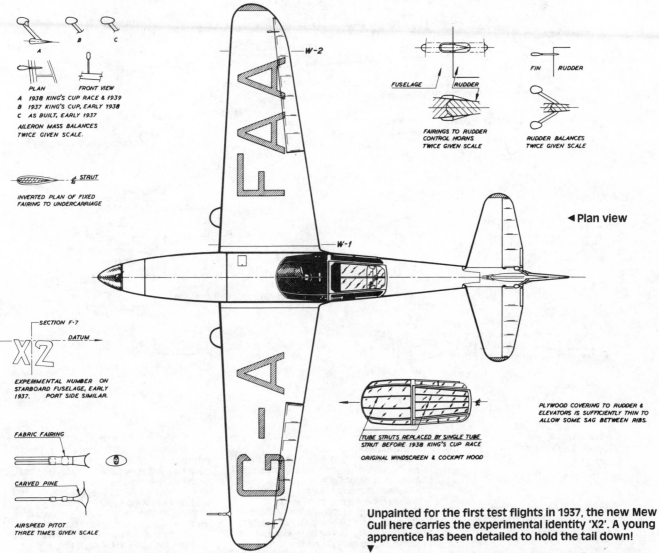

A 1938 KING'S CUP RACE & 1939
B 1937 KING'S CUP, EARLY 1938
C AS BUILT, EARLY 1937

AILERON MASS BALANCES
TWICE GIVEN SCALE.

PLAN   FRONT VIEW

INVERTED PLAN OF FIXED
FAIRING TO UNDERCARRIAGE

SECTION F-7
DATUM

EXPERIMENTAL NUMBER ON
STARBOARD FUSELAGE, EARLY
1937.   PORT SIDE SIMILAR.

FABRIC FAIRING

CARVED PINE

AIRSPEED PITOT
THREE TIMES GIVEN SCALE

W-2

W-1

FUSELAGE   RUDDER

FAIRINGS TO RUDDER
CONTROL HORNS
TWICE GIVEN SCALE

FIN   RUDDER

RUDDER BALANCES
TWICE GIVEN SCALE

◄ Plan view

PLYWOOD COVERING TO RUDDER &
ELEVATORS IS SUFFICIENTLY THIN TO
ALLOW SOME SAG BETWEEN RIBS.

TUBE STRUTS REPLACED BY SINGLE TUBE
STRUT BEFORE 1938 KING'S CUP RACE

ORIGINAL WINDSCREEN & COCKPIT HOOD

Unpainted for the first test flights in 1937, the new Mew Gull here carries the experimental identity 'X2'. A young apprentice has been detailed to hold the tail down!

▼

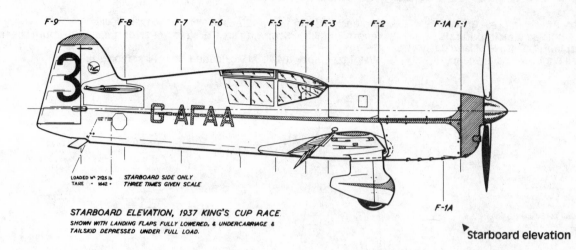

F-9 F-8 F-7 F-6 F-5 F-4 F-3 F-2 F-1A F-1

3

G·AFAA

F-1A

LOADED WT. 2125 lb   STARBOARD SIDE ONLY
TARE - 1642   THREE TIMES GIVEN SCALE

STARBOARD ELEVATION, 1937 KING'S CUP RACE.
SHOWN WITH LANDING FLAPS FULLY LOWERED, & UNDERCARRIAGE &
TAILSKID DEPRESSED UNDER FULL LOAD.

▶ **Starboard elevation**

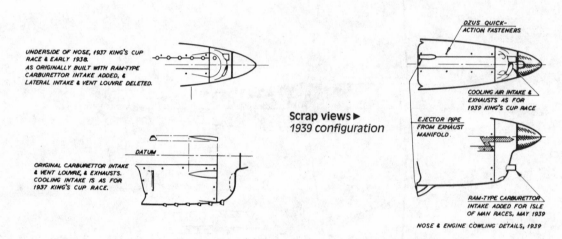

UNDERSIDE OF NOSE, 1937 KING'S CUP
RACE & EARLY 1938.
AS ORIGINALLY BUILT WITH RAM-TYPE
CARBURETTOR INTAKE ADDED, &
LATERAL INTAKE & VENT LOUVRE DELETED.

Scrap views ▶
1939 configuration

DATUM

ORIGINAL CARBURETTOR INTAKE
& VENT LOUVRE, & EXHAUSTS.
COOLING INTAKE IS AS FOR
1937 KING'S CUP RACE.

DZUS QUICK-
ACTION FASTENERS

COOLING AIR INTAKE &
EXHAUSTS AS FOR
1939 KING'S CUP RACE

EJECTOR PIPE
FROM EXHAUST
MANIFOLD.

RAM-TYPE CARBURETTOR
INTAKE ADDED FOR ISLE
OF MAN RACES, MAY 1939

NOSE & ENGINE COWLING DETAILS, 1939

Scrap views ▲
1937 King's Cup Air Race

SKY _ _ _ _ _ TURQUOISE
GULL & CLOUD _ _ _ _WHITE
OUTER RING _ _ _ _ GOLD
SEA, WING TIPS, _ _ _ DARK
& "MEW GULL". _ _ _ BLUE

PERCIVAL EMBLEM ON BOTH SIDES OF FIN FOR
1937 & 1939 ONLY.   THREE TIMES GIVEN SCALE.

Colour notes
As built, early 1937: Wings, fuselage and tail
– oxide primer; engine cowling, propeller,
wheel spats, strut fairings – natural
duralumin; ailerons – clear doped fabric;
'X2' experimental number – white.
1937 King's Cup Air Race: Entire aircraft –
off-white; all striping, registration letters,
tips of surfaces – bright blue with thin gold
outline; racing number on fin/rudder –
black.
Early 1938: As 1937 King's Cup Air Race but

with oxide primer on engine cowling and
wheel spats.
1938 King's Cup Air Race: As 1937 Race but
with modified striping, blue spinner,
Percival emblem and blue tip of fin deleted,
and altered racing number.
1939 Isle of Man Races: As 1938 Race but
with blue wing and tailplane tips deleted,
restored Percival emblem on fin and
further alteration to racing number. Rear
faces of propeller blades were black on all
versions.

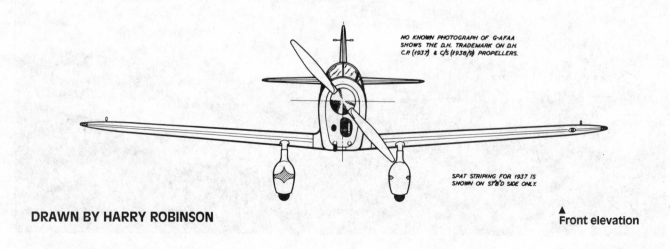

NO KNOWN PHOTOGRAPH OF G-AFAA
SHOWS THE D.H. TRADEMARK ON D.H.
C.P. (1937) & C/S (1938/9) PROPELLERS.

SPAT STRIPING FOR 1937 IS
SHOWN ON STB'D SIDE ONLY.

DRAWN BY HARRY ROBINSON

▲ **Front elevation**

▲ Cavorting in the skies above Bedfordshire during June 1939, when the racing number was 20.

IRREGULAR FORM OF RACING NUMBERS FOR 1937 & 1938 IS AUTHENTIC.

STARBOARD RACING NUMBER FOR 1938 KING'S CUP RACE

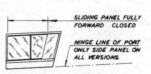

SLIDING PANEL FULLY FORWARD   CLOSED

HINGE LINE OF PORT ONLY SIDE PANEL ON ALL VERSIONS.

SLIDING PANEL TO COCKPIT HOOD, 1939.

RACING NUMBER FOR 1939 WITH PERCIVAL EMBLEM ON FIN.   STARBOARD SIDE IS SIMILAR.

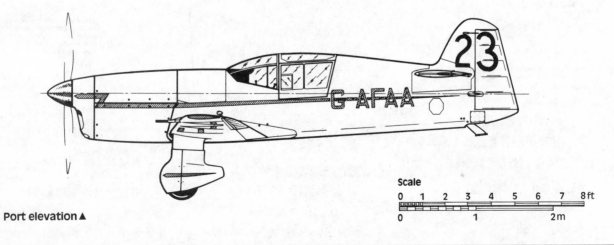

Port elevation ▲

Scale

0 1 2 3 4 5 6 7 8 ft

0   1   2 m

Scale

```
0   1   2   3   4   5   6   7   8 ft
0               1                2m
```

Notes

This drawing shows the 1938 King's Cup version of G-AFAA, Capt Edgar Percival's Mew Gull E3H (the type number 'P6A' is not correct). Earlier and later versions are shown in the scrap views. All other Mew Gulls differed considerably in wing planform and in numerous details

▲ At Hatfield in 1937 for the King's Cup, when flown by Captain Edgar Percival. It was fastest to Dublin and return but placed 2nd on handicap. Six aircraft were made, and 'EXF (Major Miller's and Alex Henshaw's) survives with Des Penrose at Old Warden.

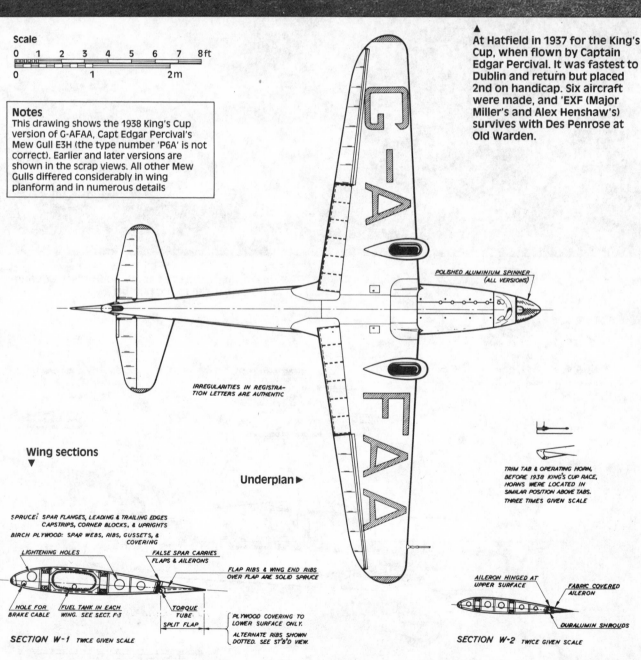

POLISHED ALUMINIUM SPINNER (ALL VERSIONS)

IRREGULARITIES IN REGISTRATION LETTERS ARE AUTHENTIC

Wing sections
▼

Underplan ►

TRIM TAB & OPERATING HORN, BEFORE 1938 KING'S CUP RACE, HORNS WERE LOCATED IN SIMILAR POSITION ABOVE TABS. THREE TIMES GIVEN SCALE

SPRUCE: SPAR FLANGES, LEADING & TRAILING EDGES CAPSTRIPS, CORNER BLOCKS, & UPRIGHTS
BIRCH PLYWOOD: SPAR WEBS, RIBS, GUSSETS, & COVERING

LIGHTENING HOLES

FALSE SPAR CARRIES FLAPS & AILERONS

FLAP RIBS & WING END RIBS OVER FLAP ARE SOLID SPRUCE

HOLE FOR BRAKE CABLE

FUEL TANK IN EACH WING. SEE SECT. F-3

TORQUE TUBE
SPLIT FLAP

PLYWOOD COVERING TO LOWER SURFACE ONLY.
ALTERNATE RIBS SHOWN DOTTED. SEE ST'B'D VIEW.

SECTION W-1 TWICE GIVEN SCALE

AILERON HINGED AT UPPER SURFACE
FABRIC COVERED AILERON
DURALUMIN SHROUDS

SECTION W-2 TWICE GIVEN SCALE

Scrap views ▶
Cockpit details

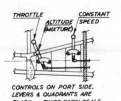

THROTTLE
ALTITUDE (MIXTURE)
CONSTANT SPEED

CONTROLS ON PORT SIDE.
LEVERS & QUADRANTS ARE
BLACK. TWICE GIVEN SCALE

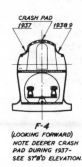

CRASH PAD
1937   1938 9

F-4
(LOOKING FORWARD)
NOTE DEEPER CRASH
PAD DURING 1937—
SEE ST'B'D ELEVATION.

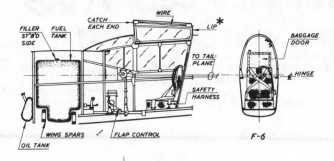

FILLER ST'B'D SIDE
FUEL TANK
CATCH EACH END
WIRE
LIP *
TO TAIL-PLANE
SAFETY HARNESS
OIL TANK
WING SPARS
FLAP CONTROL

BAGGAGE DOOR
HINGE

F-6

TRIM WHEEL & LABEL
THREE TIMES GIVEN SCALE

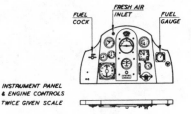

FUEL COCK
FRESH AIR INLET
FUEL GAUGE

INSTRUMENT PANEL
& ENGINE CONTROLS
TWICE GIVEN SCALE

PLAN & REAR VIEW OF
COMPASS & MOUNTING.
TWICE GIVEN SCALE.

BRAKE PEDAL
SEAT ANCHOR
PARACHUTE RIPCORD

WHERE CONVENIENT, ITEMS
AHEAD OF SECTION PLANES
ARE SHOWN IN FULL LINE.

* LIP ½" WIDE AT ENDS OF
TOP & SIDE PANELS OF
COCKPIT HOOD & FREE
EDGE OF TOP PANEL.

INTERIOR OF COCKPIT IS FINISHED MATT LIGHT GREEN ON ALL SURFACES
DECKING BENEATH WINDSCREEN IS MATT BLACK, AS ARE CRASH PAD & GRIP OF
CONTROL COLUMN. COLUMN & RUDDER & BRAKE PEDALS ARE NATURAL METAL.
CAPT. PERCIVAL'S HAT WAS DARK BROWN.

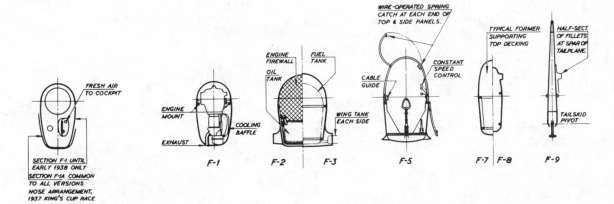

FRESH AIR TO COCKPIT

SECTION F-1 UNTIL
EARLY 1938 ONLY
SECTION F-1A COMMON
TO ALL VERSIONS
NOSE ARRANGEMENT,
1937 KING'S CUP RACE

ENGINE MOUNT
EXHAUST
COOLING BAFFLE

F-1

ENGINE FIREWALL
OIL TANK
FUEL TANK
WING TANK EACH SIDE

F-2   **F-3**

WIRE-OPERATED SPRING
CATCH AT EACH END OF
TOP & SIDE PANELS.

CABLE GUIDE
CONSTANT SPEED CONTROL

F-5

TYPICAL FORMER
SUPPORTING
TOP DECKING

HALF-SECT.
OF FILLETS
AT SPAR OF
TAILPLANE.

TAILSKID PIVOT

F-7 **F-8**   **F-9**

Fuselage cross-sections ▲

In 1938 scheme, racing with Captain Percival its designer
as number 23, the E3H had a potential of 264mph but the
sixty turns within the race slowed it considerably.
▼

Rollason Beta Types B1, B2 and B4

Country of origin: Great Britain.
Type: Single-seat racing aircraft.
Powerplant: One Continental A-65 engine rated at 65hp, (B2) Continental C-90 rated at 90hp, (B4) 0-200A rated at 100hp.
Dimensions: Wing span 20ft 5in *6.22m*;
length 16ft 8in *5.08m*, (with propeller extension) 17ft 0in *5.18m*; height 4ft 10in *1.47m*; wing area 66 sq ft *6.13m²*.
Weights: Empty 565lb *256kg*; maximum 875lb *397kg*.
Performance: Maximum speed 165mph *266kph*, (B2) 200mph *322kph*, (B4)
180mph *290kph*; climb rate 1100ft/min *335m/min*, (B2) 2000ft/min *610m/min*, (B4) 1500ft/min *460m/min*; range 350 miles *563km*, (B2) 310 miles *500km*, (B4) 500 miles *805km*.
First flight: (Prototype) 1966.

DRAWN BY A A P LLOYD

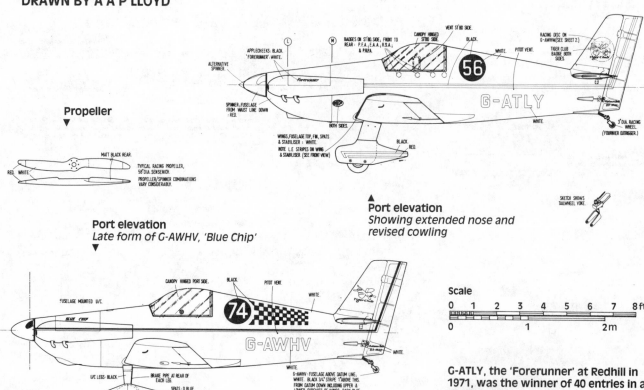

Propeller ▼

Port elevation
Late form of G-AWHV, 'Blue Chip' ▼

Port elevation
Showing extended nose and revised cowling

Scale

```
0   1   2   3   4   5   6   7   8 ft
0           1              2 m
```

G-ATLY, the 'Forerunner' at Redhill in 1971, was the winner of 40 entries in a design contest for a VW-engined racer of 65 sq ft wing area. Fitted with a 65hp Continental, the aircraft had a flyaway price of £3750 (R G Moulton)

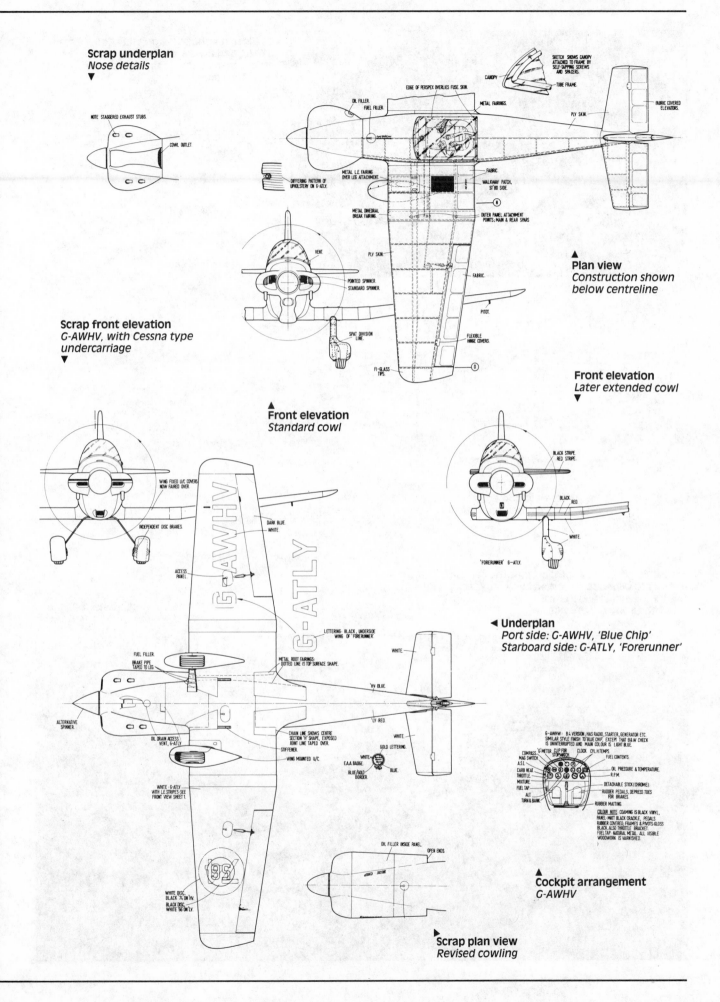

Scrap underplan
Nose details
▼

NOTE STAGGERED EXHAUST STUBS.

COWL OUTLET

Scrap front elevation
G-AWHV, with Cessna type undercarriage
▼

SKETCH SHOWS CANOPY ATTACHED TO FRAME BY SELF-TAPPING SCREWS AND SPACERS.

CANOPY

TUBE FRAME

EDGE OF PERSPEX OVERLIES FUSE. SKIN

OIL FILLER.
FUEL FILLER.

METAL FAIRINGS.

FABRIC COVERED ELEVATORS.

PLY SKIN.

FABRIC.

METAL L.E. FAIRING OVER LEG ATTACHMENT.

WALKWAY PATCH, ST'BD SIDE.

METAL DIHEDRAL BREAK FAIRING.

OUTER PANEL ATTACHMENT POINTS; MAIN & REAR SPARS.

VENT.

PLY SKIN.

POINTED SPINNER.
STANDARD SPINNER.

FABRIC.

PITOT.

SPAT DIVISION LINE.

FLEXIBLE HINGE COVERS.

FI-GLASS TIPS.

DIFFERING PATTERN OF UPHOLSTERY ON G-ATLY.

▲ Plan view
Construction shown below centreline

Front elevation
Standard cowl
▲

WING FIXED U/C COVERS NOW FAIRED OVER.

INDEPENDENT DISC BRAKES.

ACCESS PANEL.

Front elevation
Later extended cowl
▼

BLACK STRIPE.
RED STRIPE.

BLACK.
RED.

WHITE.

'FORERUNNER' G-ATLY.

◄ Underplan
Port side: G-AWHV, 'Blue Chip'
Starboard side: G-ATLY, 'Forerunner'

G-AWHV

G-ATLY

DARK BLUE
WHITE

FUEL FILLER.
BRAKE PIPE TAPED TO LEG.

METAL ROOT FAIRINGS; DOTTED LINE IS TOP SURFACE SHAPE.

LETTERING: BLACK, UNDERSIDE WING OF 'FORERUNNER'

WHITE

'HV' BLUE

'LY' RED.

WHITE.

ALTERNATIVE SPINNER.

OIL DRAIN ACCESS VENT, G-ATLY

CHAIN LINE SHOWS CENTRE SECTION 'N' SHAPE, EXPOSED JOINT LINE TAPED OVER.

STIFFENER.

WING MOUNTED U/C.

GOLD LETTERING.

WHITE.
E.A.A. BADGE.
BLUE/GOLD BORDER.

BLUE.

WHITE G-ATLY WITH L.E. STRIPES; SEE FRONT VIEW SHEET 1.

WHITE DISC, BLACK '74 ON HV.
BLACK DISC, WHITE '56 ON LY.

OIL FILLER INSIDE PANEL.

OPEN ENDS.

▲ Scrap plan view
Revised cowling

G-AWHV: B.4 VERSION, HAS RADIO, STARTER, GENERATOR ETC. SIMILAR STYLE FINISH TO 'BLUE CHIP', EXCEPT THAT B&W CHECK IS UNINTERRUPTED AND MAIN COLOUR IS LIGHT BLUE.

COMPASS.
MAG SWITCH
A.S.I.
CARB HEAT
THROTTLE
MIXTURE
FUEL TAP
ALT
TURN & BANK

G'METER CLIP FOR STOPWATCH

CLOCK. CYL. H.TEMPS

FUEL CONTENTS.

OIL PRESSURE & TEMPERATURE.

R.P.M.

DETACHABLE STICK (CHROME).

RUDDER PEDALS, DEPRESS TOES FOR BRAKES.

RUBBER MATTING.

COLOUR NOTE: COAMING IS BLACK VINYL, PANEL MATT BLACK CRACKLE. PEDALS RUBBER COVERED, FRAMES & PIVOTS-GLOSS BLACK, ALSO THROTTLE BRACKET. FUELTAP NATURAL METAL. ALL VISIBLE WOODWORK IS VARNISHED.

▲ Cockpit arrangement
G-AWHV

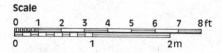

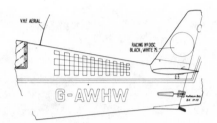

◄ The instrument panel on 'Blue Chip', Beta G-AWHV, and a view of the high quality, yacht-style construction of the curvaceous fuselage. (R G Moulton)

Scale

```
0  1   2   3   4   5   6   7   8ft
0              1              2m
```

Wing sections ▲

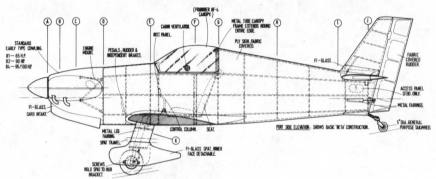

Port elevation ▲
Showing basic construction

'Blue Chip', here on approach, was the second aircraft to be made, followed by 'Dandy Dick', G-AWHW. Cowlings were considerably modified through racing experience.
▼

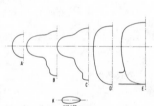

Fuselage cross-sections

Supermarine S5

Country of origin: Great Britain.
Type: Single-seat racing seaplane.
Powerplant: One Napier Lion VII engine rated at 875hp.
Dimensions: Wing span 26ft 9in *8.15m*;

length 24ft 2½in *7.38m*; wing area 115 sq ft *10.68m²*.
Weights: Empty (Lion VIID) 2602lb *1180kg*, (Lion VIIG) 2536lb *1150kg*; loaded (VIID) 3043lb *1380kg*, (VIIG) 3197lb *1450kg*.

Performance: Maximum speed (record) 319.5mph *514.4kph*.
First flight: August 1927.

Starboard elevation
▼

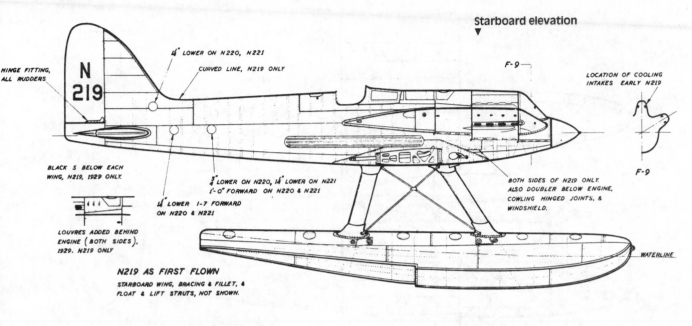

HINGE FITTING, ALL RUDDERS

4" LOWER ON N220, N221

CURVED LINE, N219 ONLY

F-9

LOCATION OF COOLING INTAKES EARLY N219

BLACK S BELOW EACH WING, N219, 1929 ONLY.

¾" LOWER ON N220, 1¼" LOWER ON N221 1'-0" FORWARD ON N220 & N221

F-9

1¼" LOWER 1-7 FORWARD ON N220 & N221

BOTH SIDES OF N219 ONLY. ALSO DOUBLER BELOW ENGINE, COWLING HINGED JOINTS, & WINDSHIELD.

LOUVRES ADDED BEHIND ENGINE (BOTH SIDES). 1929. N219 ONLY

WATERLINE

N219 AS FIRST FLOWN
STARBOARD WING, BRACING & FILLET, & FLOAT & LIFT STRUTS, NOT SHOWN.

Scale

0 1 2 3 4 5 6 7 8 ft

0   1   2m

Flt Lt D'Arcy-Grieg stands in the tiny cockpit of the first S5 in 1929 at Calshot where it was used for training.
▼

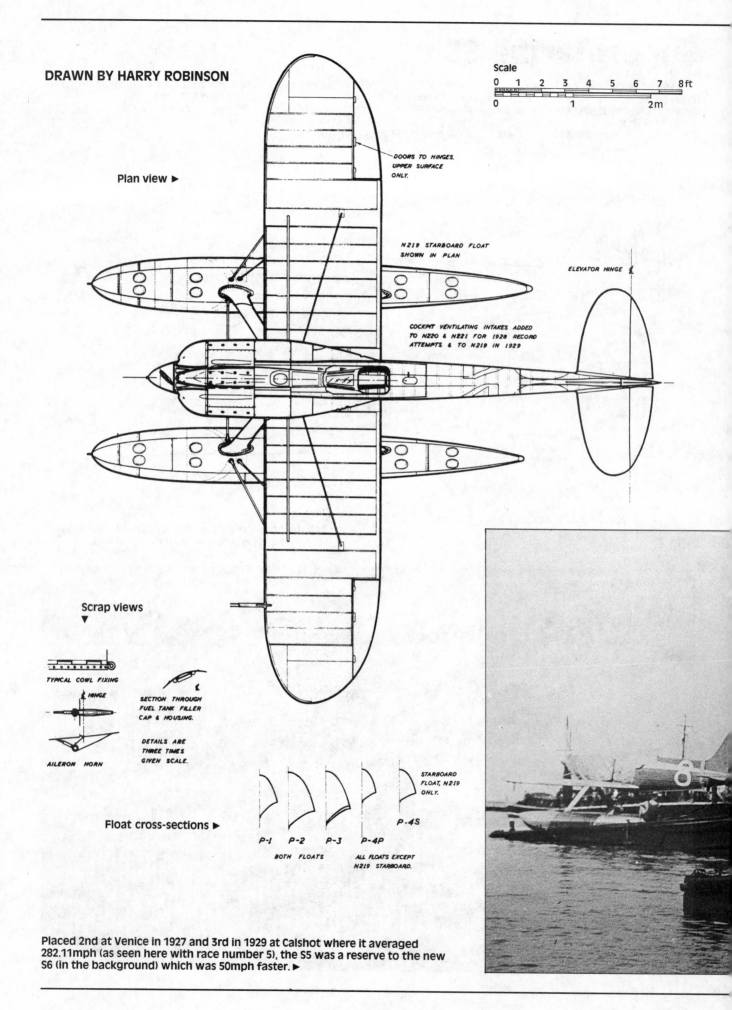

DRAWN BY HARRY ROBINSON

Scale

Plan view ▶

DOORS TO HINGES.
UPPER SURFACE
ONLY.

N 219 STARBOARD FLOAT
SHOWN IN PLAN

ELEVATOR HINGE

COCKPIT VENTILATING INTAKES ADDED
TO N220 & N221 FOR 1928 RECORD
ATTEMPTS & TO N219 IN 1929

Scrap views
▼

TYPICAL COWL FIXING

HINGE

SECTION THROUGH
FUEL TANK FILLER
CAP & HOUSING.

DETAILS ARE
THREE TIMES
GIVEN SCALE.

AILERON HORN

STARBOARD
FLOAT, N219
ONLY.

Float cross-sections ▶

P-1   P-2   P-3   P-4P   P-4S

BOTH FLOATS   ALL FLOATS EXCEPT
N219 STARBOARD.

**Placed 2nd at Venice in 1927 and 3rd in 1929 at Calshot where it averaged
282.11mph (as seen here with race number 5), the S5 was a reserve to the new
S6 (in the background) which was 50mph faster. ▶**

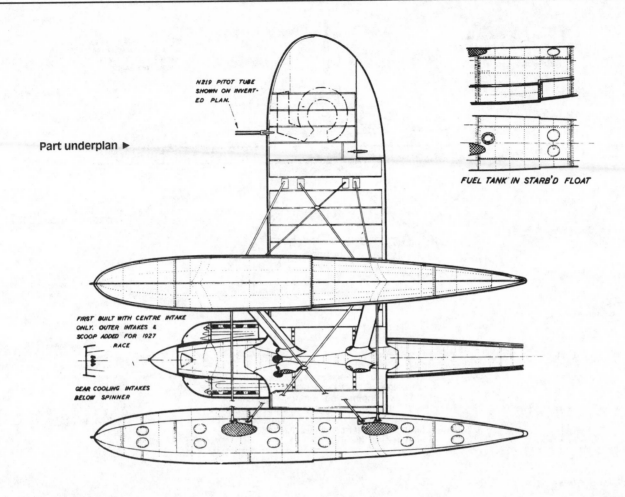

Part underplan ▶

N219 PITOT TUBE SHOWN ON INVERTED PLAN.

FUEL TANK IN STARB'D FLOAT

FIRST BUILT WITH CENTRE INTAKE ONLY. OUTER INTAKES & SCOOP ADDED FOR 1927 RACE

GEAR COOLING INTAKES BELOW SPINNER

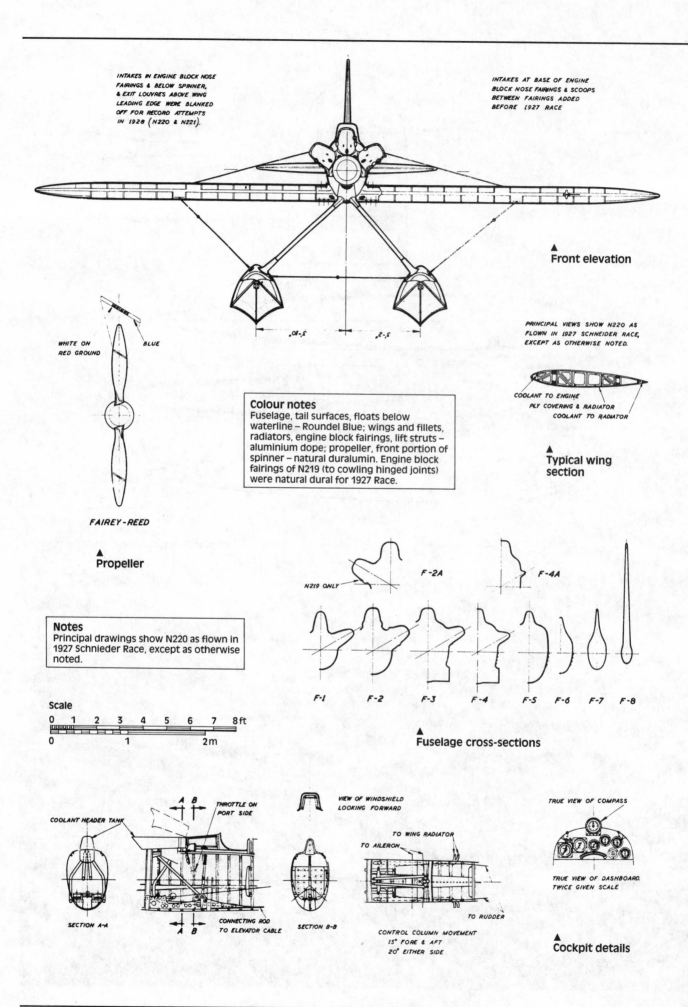

INTAKES IN ENGINE BLOCK NOSE
FAIRINGS & BELOW SPINNER,
& EXIT LOUVRES ABOVE WING
LEADING EDGE WERE BLANKED
OFF FOR RECORD ATTEMPTS
IN 1928 (N220 & N221).

INTAKES AT BASE OF ENGINE
BLOCK NOSE FAIRINGS & SCOOPS
BETWEEN FAIRINGS ADDED
BEFORE 1927 RACE

▲ Front elevation

PRINCIPAL VIEWS SHOW N220 AS
FLOWN IN 1927 SCHNEIDER RACE,
EXCEPT AS OTHERWISE NOTED.

WHITE ON
RED GROUND

BLUE

COOLANT TO ENGINE
PLY COVERING & RADIATOR
COOLANT TO RADIATOR

▲ Typical wing
section

Colour notes
Fuselage, tail surfaces, floats below
waterline – Roundel Blue; wings and fillets,
radiators, engine block fairings, lift struts –
aluminium dope; propeller, front portion of
spinner – natural duralumin. Engine block
fairings of N219 (to cowling hinged joints)
were natural dural for 1927 Race.

FAIREY - REED

▲ Propeller

N219 ONLY

F-2A

F-4A

Notes
Principal drawings show N220 as flown in
1927 Schnieder Race, except as otherwise
noted.

F-1   F-2   F-3   F-4   F-5   F-6   F-7   F-8

▲ Fuselage cross-sections

Scale

0 1 2 3 4 5 6 7 8 ft

0   1   2 m

COOLANT HEADER TANK

A B

THROTTLE ON
PORT SIDE

VIEW OF WINDSHIELD
LOOKING FORWARD

TRUE VIEW OF COMPASS

TO WING RADIATOR

TO AILERON

TRUE VIEW OF DASHBOARD.
TWICE GIVEN SCALE

SECTION A-A

A B

CONNECTING ROD
TO ELEVATOR CABLE

SECTION B-B

TO RUDDER

CONTROL COLUMN MOVEMENT
15° FORE & AFT
20° EITHER SIDE

▲ Cockpit details

▲
At Venice in 1927, N220, the second of three S5s, won the race, despite a loose cowling, at 281.54mph; it was flown by Flt Lt S N Webster. Still conditions at the Lido are evident from the vertical smoke plume.

Scrap views ▶
N219, Schneider Race

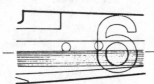

1927 SCHNEIDER RACE

1929 SCHNEIDER RACE
NOTE LOCATION OF CIRCULAR INSPECTION DOORS
NO RACING NUMBERS OP ROUNDELS ON N221

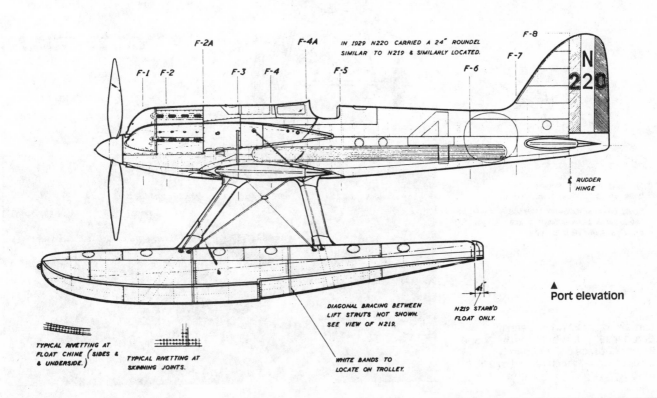

F-1 F-2 F-2A F-3 F-4 F-4A F-5 F-6 F-7 F-8

IN 1929 N220 CARRIED A 24" ROUNDEL
SIMILAR TO N219 & SIMILARLY LOCATED.

N 220

RUDDER HINGE

▲ **Port elevation**

DIAGONAL BRACING BETWEEN
LIFT STRUTS NOT SHOWN.
SEE VIEW OF N219.

N219 STARB'D
FLOAT ONLY.

TYPICAL RIVETTING AT
FLOAT CHINE (SIDES &
& UNDERSIDE.)

TYPICAL RIVETTING AT
SKINNING JOINTS.

WHITE BANDS TO
LOCATE ON TROLLEY.

Bernard V2

Country of origin: France.
Type: Single-seat racing aircraft.
Powerplant: One Hispano-Suiza Type 50 'W' engine rated at 450hp.
Dimensions: Wing span (Oct 1924) 32ft

5³⁄₄in *9.90m*, (Dec 1924) 29ft 10¼in *9.10m*; length 22ft 3³⁄₄in *6.80m*; wing area (Oct 1924) 125 sq ft *11.6m²*, (Dec 1924) 116 sq ft *10.8m²*.
Weights: Empty 2099lb *952kg*; loaded

(Oct 1924) 2608lb *1183kg*, (Dec 1924) 2646lb *1200kg*.
Performance: Maximum speed (record) 278.4mph *448.17kph*.
First flight: Summer 1924.

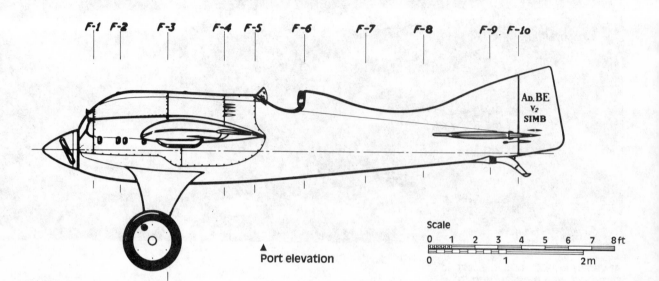

F-1 F-2   F-3   F-4 F-5   F-6   F-7   F-8   F-9 F-10

Ad. BE
V2
SIMB

▲ Port elevation

Scale
0 1 2 3 4 5 6 7 8 ft
0   1   2m

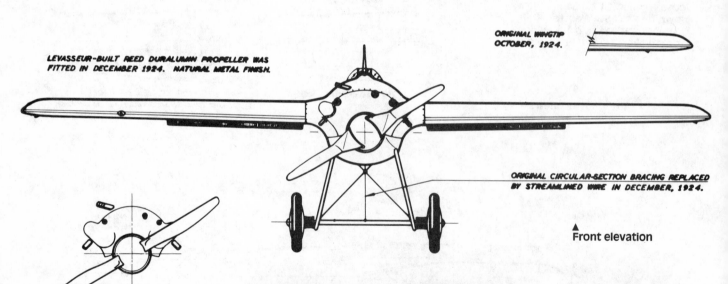

ORIGINAL WINGTIP OCTOBER, 1924.

LEVASSEUR-BUILT REED DURALUMIN PROPELLER WAS FITTED IN DECEMBER 1924. NATURAL METAL FINISH.

ORIGINAL CIRCULAR-SECTION BRACING REPLACED BY STREAMLINED WIRE IN DECEMBER, 1924.

▲ Front elevation

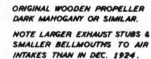

ORIGINAL WOODEN PROPELLER DARK MAHOGANY OR SIMILAR.

NOTE LARGER EXHAUST STUBS & SMALLER BELLMOUTHS TO AIR INTAKES THAN IN DEC. 1924.

Bernard racer V2 No 02, seen in October 1924, was built for the Coupé Beaumont race and ultimately established a French record of 278. 3 mph.▶

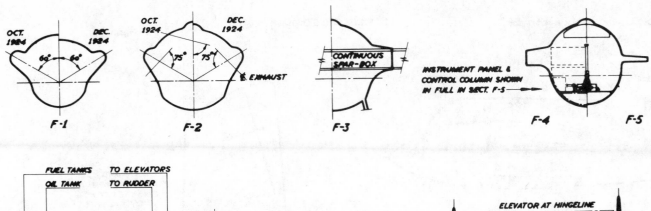

F-1 F-2 F-3 F-4 F-5

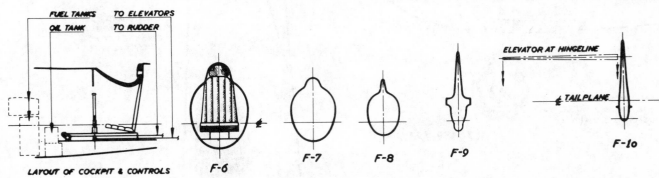

LAYOUT OF COCKPIT & CONTROLS F-6 F-7 F-8 F-9 F-10

▲ Fuselage cross-sections

◄ Scrap views
Cockpit details

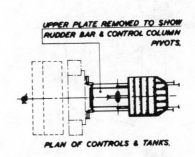

UPPER PLATE REMOVED TO SHOW RUDDER BAR & CONTROL COLUMN PIVOTS.

PLAN OF CONTROLS & TANKS.

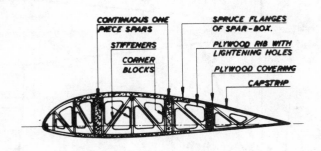

CONTINUOUS ONE PIECE SPARS
STIFFENERS
CORNER BLOCKS
SPRUCE FLANGES OF SPAR-BOX.
PLYWOOD RIB WITH LIGHTENING HOLES
PLYWOOD COVERING
CAPSTRIP

INCIDENCE
0° IN OCTOBER 1924
−3°' IN DECEMBER 1924

Wing section at root ▲
Twice given scale

SLOT FOR AXLE SHOCK TRAVEL.

DETAILS OF UNDER-CARRIAGE BRACING & AXLE MOVEMENT.
TWICE GIVEN SCALE

A rear three-quarter view of 02 emphasises the razor-like lines of the then very advanced racing design which held the world's absolute speed record for eight years. ▶

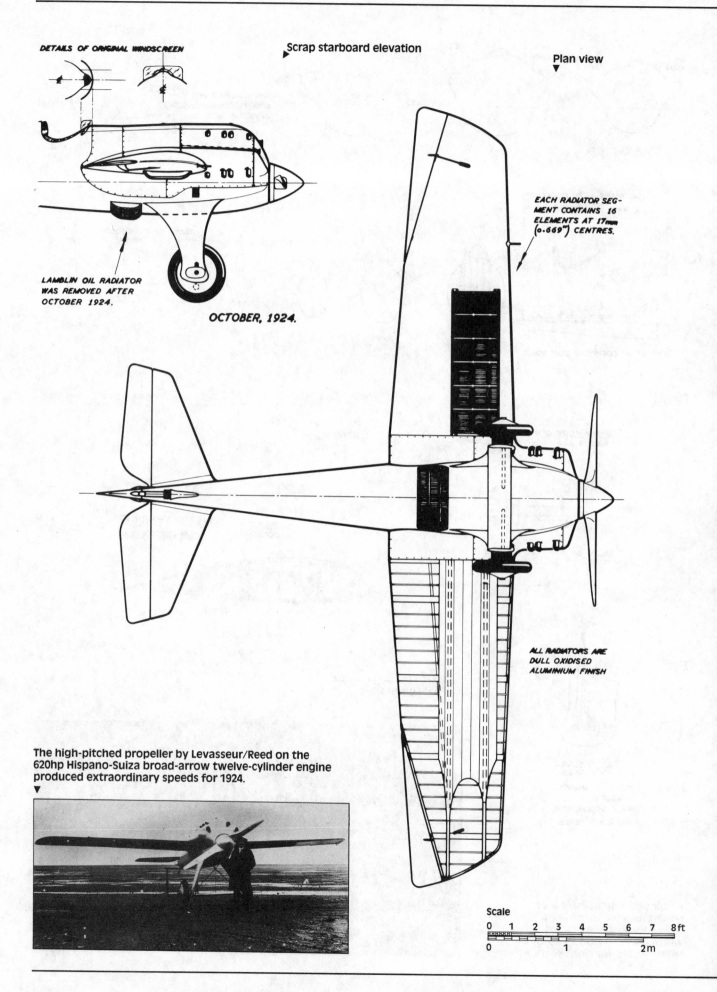

DETAILS OF ORIGINAL WINDSCREEN

Scrap starboard elevation ▶

Plan view ▼

LAMBLIN OIL RADIATOR
WAS REMOVED AFTER
OCTOBER 1924.

OCTOBER, 1924.

EACH RADIATOR SEG-
MENT CONTAINS 16
ELEMENTS AT 17mm
(0.669") CENTRES.

ALL RADIATORS ARE
DULL OXIDISED
ALUMINIUM FINISH

The high-pitched propeller by Levasseur/Reed on the
620hp Hispano-Suiza broad-arrow twelve-cylinder engine
produced extraordinary speeds for 1924.
▼

Scale

0 1 2 3 4 5 6 7 8ft

0   1   2m

DRAWN BY HARRY ROBINSON

Colour notes
Doped aluminium overall with (Oct 1924) natural metal engine cowling, spinner and wheel discs. Black legend on rudder, exhaust stubs, filler caps, air intakes, pitot tube and steel shoe of tailskid.

Underplan ▶

Notes
The drawings depict V2 No 02 only; No 01 was displayed at the 1924 Paris *Salon* and differed in many details. Port and front elevations and plan view show V2 No 02 as on 11 December 1924; the other views depict the October 1924 configuration.

DETAILS OF TANK FILLER CAPS.
FOUR TIMES GIVEN SCALE

WHEELS & TAILSKID SPRUNG BY RUBBER SHOCK-CORD.

SIMB

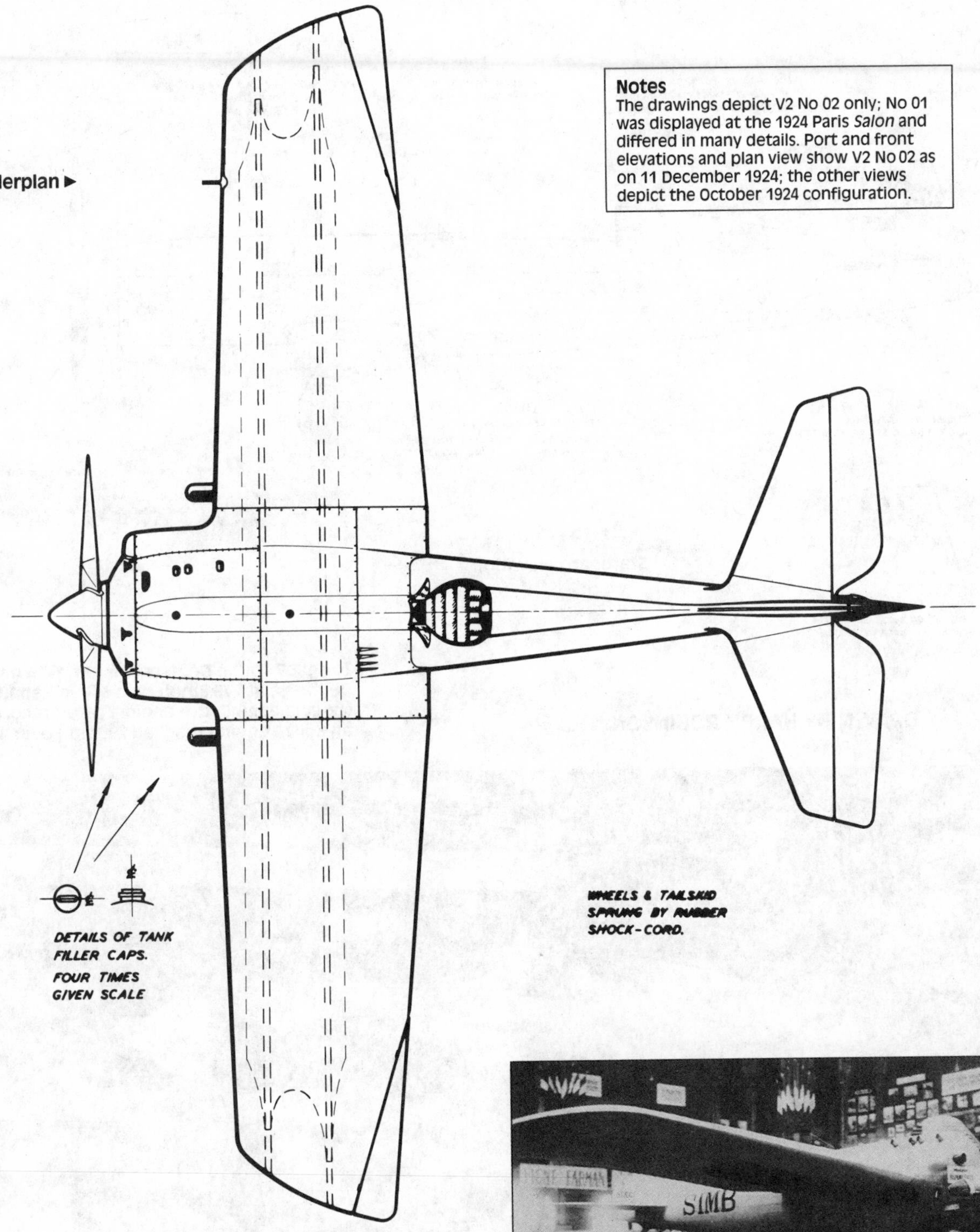

At the Paris *Salon* in 1924, 01 was named as the record holder but it certainly never flew! It differed in detail from the successful 02. ▶

Caudron C460

Country of origin: France.
Type: Single-seat racing aircraft.
Powerplant: One Renault R456 engine rated at 300–350hp.

Dimensions: Wing span 22ft 1¾in *6.75m*; length 23ft 4½in *7.12m*; wing area 75.3 sq ft *7.0m²*.
Weights: Empty 1147lb *520kg*; loaded

1984lb *900kg*.
Performance: Maximum speed about 300mph *483kph*.
First flight: 1933.

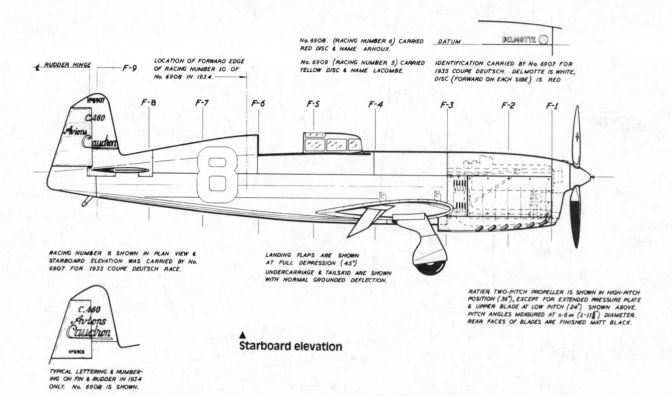

RUDDER HINGE — F-9

LOCATION OF FORWARD EDGE OF RACING NUMBER 10 OF No. 6908 IN 1934.

No. 6908. (RACING NUMBER 6) CARRIED RED DISC & NAME ARNOUX.

No. 6909 (RACING NUMBER 5) CARRIED YELLOW DISC & NAME LACOMBE.

DATUM   DELMOTTE

IDENTIFICATION CARRIED BY No. 6907 FOR 1935 COUPE DEUTSCH. DELMOTTE IS WHITE, DISC (FORWARD ON EACH SIDE) IS RED

RACING NUMBER 8 SHOWN IN PLAN VIEW & STARBOARD ELEVATION WAS CARRIED BY No. 6907 FOR 1935 COUPE DEUTSCH RACE.

LANDING FLAPS ARE SHOWN AT FULL DEPRESSION (45°) UNDERCARRIAGE & TAILSKID ARE SHOWN WITH NORMAL GROUNDED DEFLECTION.

RATIER TWO-PITCH PROPELLER IS SHOWN IN HIGH-PITCH POSITION (36°), EXCEPT FOR EXTENDED PRESSURE PLATE & UPPER BLADE AT LOW PITCH (24°) SHOWN ABOVE. PITCH ANGLES MEASURED AT 0·6m (1-11⅝) DIAMETER. REAR FACES OF BLADES ARE FINISHED MATT BLACK.

▲ **Starboard elevation**

TYPICAL LETTERING & NUMBER-ING ON FIN & RUDDER IN 1934 ONLY. No. 6908 IS SHOWN.

DRAWN BY HARRY ROBINSON

The 1935 Coupé Deutsch winner, flown by Delmotte at 275.8mph on a 330hp Renault six-cylinder 9.5-litre engine. Later, records with an 8-litre engine reached 296mph over 100km.
▼

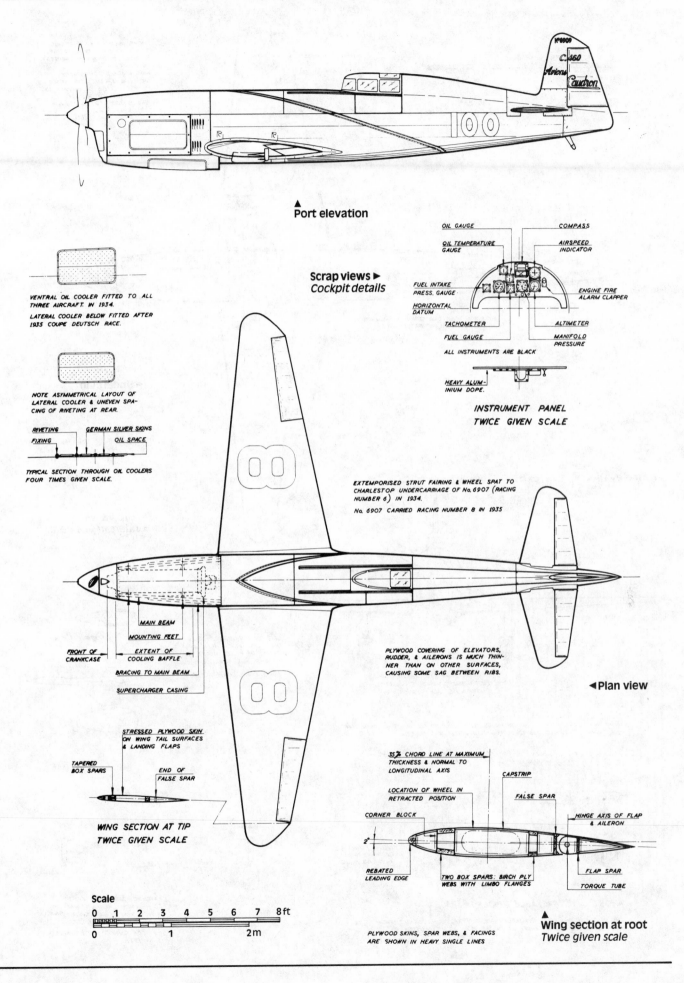

▲ Port elevation

VENTRAL OIL COOLER FITTED TO ALL THREE AIRCRAFT IN 1934.
LATERAL COOLER BELOW FITTED AFTER 1935 COUPE DEUTSCH RACE.

NOTE ASYMMETRICAL LAYOUT OF LATERAL COOLER & UNEVEN SPACING OF RIVETING AT REAR.

RIVETING   GERMAN SILVER SKINS
FIXING   OIL SPACE

TYPICAL SECTION THROUGH OIL COOLERS FOUR TIMES GIVEN SCALE.

Scrap views ▶
Cockpit details

OIL GAUGE — COMPASS
OIL TEMPERATURE GAUGE — AIRSPEED INDICATOR
FUEL INTAKE PRESS. GAUGE — ENGINE FIRE ALARM CLAPPER
HORIZONTAL DATUM
TACHOMETER — ALTIMETER
FUEL GAUGE — MANIFOLD PRESSURE

ALL INSTRUMENTS ARE BLACK

HEAVY ALUMINIUM DOPE.

INSTRUMENT PANEL
TWICE GIVEN SCALE

EXTEMPORISED STRUT FAIRING & WHEEL SPAT TO CHARLESTOP UNDERCARRIAGE OF No. 6907 (RACING NUMBER 6) IN 1934.

No. 6907 CARRIED RACING NUMBER 8 IN 1935

MAIN BEAM
MOUNTING FEET
EXTENT OF COOLING BAFFLE
FRONT OF CRANKCASE
BRACING TO MAIN BEAM
SUPERCHARGER CASING

PLYWOOD COVERING OF ELEVATORS, RUDDER, & AILERONS IS MUCH THINNER THAN ON OTHER SURFACES, CAUSING SOME SAG BETWEEN RIBS.

◀ Plan view

STRESSED PLYWOOD SKIN ON WING TAIL SURFACES & LANDING FLAPS

TAPERED BOX SPARS
END OF FALSE SPAR

WING SECTION AT TIP
TWICE GIVEN SCALE

35% CHORD LINE AT MAXIMUM THICKNESS & NORMAL TO LONGITUDINAL AXIS
CAPSTRIP
LOCATION OF WHEEL IN RETRACTED POSITION
FALSE SPAR
CORNER BLOCK
HINGE AXIS OF FLAP & AILERON
2°
REBATED LEADING EDGE
TWO BOX SPARS: BIRCH PLY WEBS WITH LIMBO FLANGES
FLAP SPAR
TORQUE TUBE

▲ Wing section at root
Twice given scale

Scale

0 1 2 3 4 5 6 7 8 ft

0 1 2m

PLYWOOD SKINS, SPAR WEBS, & FACINGS ARE SHOWN IN HEAVY SINGLE LINES

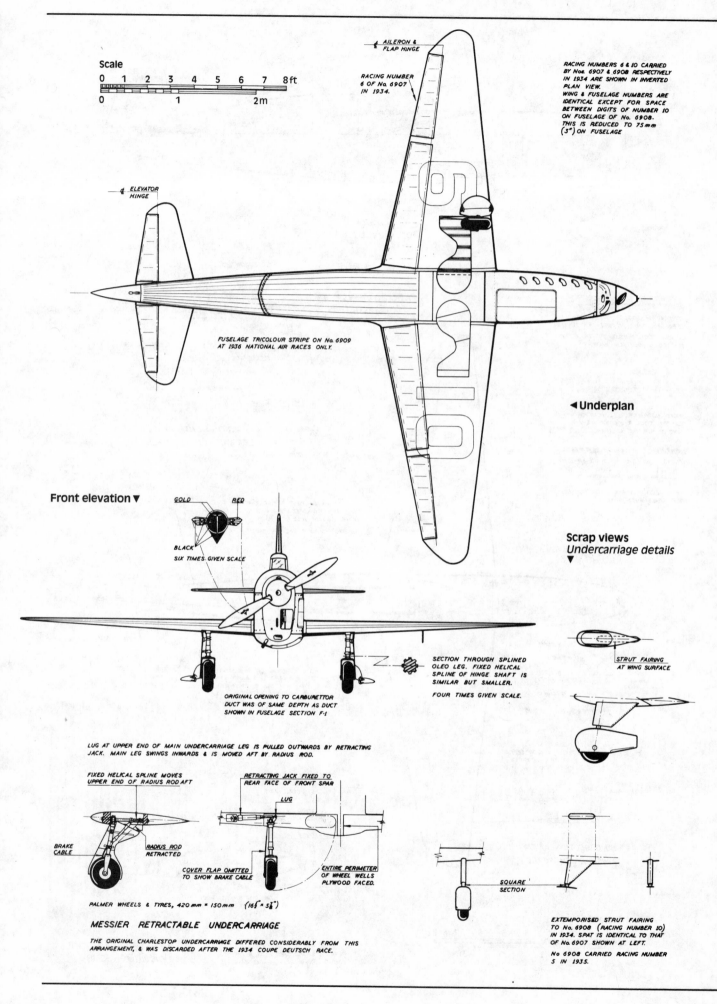

Scale

0 1 2 3 4 5 6 7 8 ft

0   1   2m

AILERON &
FLAP HINGE

RACING NUMBER
6 OF No. 6907
IN 1934.

RACING NUMBERS 6 & 10 CARRIED
BY Nos. 6907 & 6908 RESPECTIVELY
IN 1934 ARE SHOWN IN INVERTED
PLAN VIEW.
WING & FUSELAGE NUMBERS ARE
IDENTICAL EXCEPT FOR SPACE
BETWEEN DIGITS OF NUMBER 10
ON FUSELAGE OF No. 6908.
THIS IS REDUCED TO 75 mm
(3") ON FUSELAGE

ELEVATOR
HINGE

FUSELAGE TRICOLOUR STRIPE ON No. 6909
AT 1936 NATIONAL AIR RACES ONLY.

◄ Underplan

Front elevation ▼

GOLD   RED

BLACK

SIX TIMES GIVEN SCALE

Scrap views
Undercarriage details
▼

SECTION THROUGH SPLINED
OLEO LEG. FIXED HELICAL
SPLINE OF HINGE SHAFT IS
SIMILAR BUT SMALLER.

FOUR TIMES GIVEN SCALE.

ORIGINAL OPENING TO CARBURETTOR
DUCT WAS OF SAME DEPTH AS DUCT
SHOWN IN FUSELAGE SECTION F-1

STRUT FAIRING
AT WING SURFACE

LUG AT UPPER END OF MAIN UNDERCARRIAGE LEG IS PULLED OUTWARDS BY RETRACTING
JACK. MAIN LEG SWINGS INWARDS & IS MOVED AFT BY RADIUS ROD.

FIXED HELICAL SPLINE MOVES
UPPER END OF RADIUS ROD AFT

RETRACTING JACK FIXED TO
REAR FACE OF FRONT SPAR

LUG

BRAKE
CABLE

RADIUS ROD
RETRACTED

COVER FLAP OMITTED
TO SHOW BRAKE CABLE

ENTIRE PERIMETER
OF WHEEL WELLS
PLYWOOD FACED.

SQUARE
SECTION

PALMER WHEELS & TYRES, 420 mm × 150 mm (16⅝" × 5⅞")

MESSIER RETRACTABLE UNDERCARRIAGE

THE ORIGINAL CHARLESTOP UNDERCARRIAGE DIFFERED CONSIDERABLY FROM THIS
ARRANGEMENT, & WAS DISCARDED AFTER THE 1934 COUPE DEUTSCH RACE.

EXTEMPORISED STRUT FAIRING
TO No. 6908 (RACING NUMBER 10)
IN 1934. SPAT IS IDENTICAL TO THAT
OF No. 6907 SHOWN AT LEFT.

No. 6908 CARRIED RACING NUMBER
5 IN 1935.

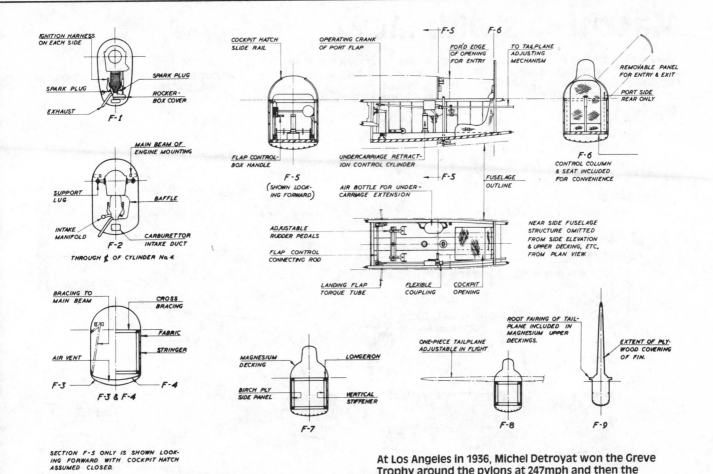

F-1
IGNITION HARNESS ON EACH SIDE
SPARK PLUG
SPARK PLUG
ROCKER-BOX COVER
EXHAUST

F-2
MAIN BEAM OF ENGINE MOUNTING
SUPPORT LUG
BAFFLE
INTAKE MANIFOLD
CARBURETTOR INTAKE DUCT
THROUGH ₵ OF CYLINDER No. 4.

F-3 & F-4
BRACING TO MAIN BEAM
CROSS BRACING
FABRIC
STRINGER
AIR VENT
F-3
F-4

SECTION F-5 ONLY IS SHOWN LOOKING FORWARD WITH COCKPIT HATCH ASSUMED CLOSED.

F-5
COCKPIT HATCH SLIDE RAIL
FLAP CONTROL-BOX HANDLE
F-5 (SHOWN LOOKING FORWARD)

OPERATING CRANK OF PORT FLAP
FOR'D EDGE OF OPENING FOR ENTRY
TO TAILPLANE ADJUSTING MECHANISM
F-5
F-6
UNDERCARRIAGE RETRACTION CONTROL CYLINDER
F-5
FUSELAGE OUTLINE

AIR BOTTLE FOR UNDERCARRIAGE EXTENSION
ADJUSTABLE RUDDER PEDALS
FLAP CONTROL CONNECTING ROD
LANDING FLAP TORQUE TUBE
FLEXIBLE COUPLING
COCKPIT OPENING

F-6
REMOVABLE PANEL FOR ENTRY & EXIT
PORT SIDE REAR ONLY
CONTROL COLUMN & SEAT INCLUDED FOR CONVENIENCE
NEAR SIDE FUSELAGE STRUCTURE OMITTED FROM SIDE ELEVATION & UPPER DECKING, ETC., FROM PLAN VIEW.

F-7
MAGNESIUM DECKING
LONGERON
BIRCH PLY SIDE PANEL
VERTICAL STIFFENER

F-8
ONE-PIECE TAILPLANE ADJUSTABLE IN FLIGHT
ROOT FAIRING OF TAILPLANE INCLUDED IN MAGNESIUM UPPER DECKINGS.

F-9
EXTENT OF PLYWOOD COVERING OF FIN.

Fuselage cross-sections ▲

At Los Angeles in 1936, Michel Detroyat won the Greve Trophy around the pylons at 247mph and then the Thompson Trophy at an average of 264mph over 150 miles to achieve time-honoured fame. The best lap was at 301mph.
▼

Macchi-Castoldi MC72

Country of origin: Italy.
Type: Single-seat racing seaplane.
Powerplant: One Fiat AS-6 24-cylinder inline engine rated at 2800hp.

Dimensions: Wing span 31ft 1½in *9.49m*; length 28ft 3in *8.61m*; wing area 161.5 sq ft *150m²*.
Weights: Empty 5512lb *2500kg*; loaded

6410lb *2907kg*.
Performance: Maximum speed (record) 440.68mph *709kph*.
First flight: 1931.

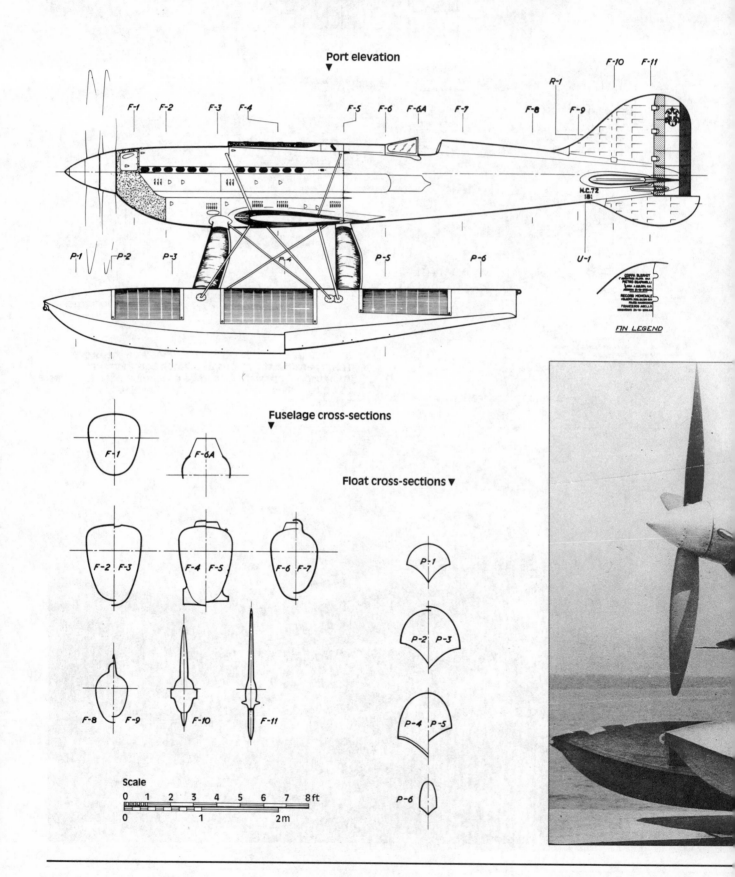

Port elevation ▼

Fuselage cross-sections ▼

Float cross-sections ▼

FIN LEGEND

Scale
0 1 2 3 4 5 6 7 8ft
0 1 2m

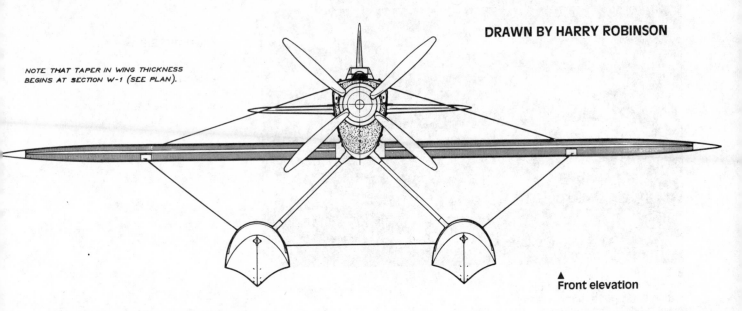

DRAWN BY HARRY ROBINSON

NOTE THAT TAPER IN WING THICKNESS
BEGINS AT SECTION W-1 (SEE PLAN).

▲
Front elevation

Notes
These drawings show No 181 as it appeared
at the 1934 Paris *Salon* following the record
of 23 October that year. Present
modifications include shortened underfin
and minor changes to paint finish. Nos 179
and 180 were fitted with longer floats and
ventral coolant radiator but did not
originally have either the extended
underfin or the tunnel carburettor intake.

The MC72 was built for the Fiat AS6 tandem dual engine
unit of 3100hp to race the S6B in 1931 but development
problems, including a fateful spin into Lake Garda,
precluded race participation. Tests had shown it capable
of 375mph before a second MC72 crashed fatally.
▼

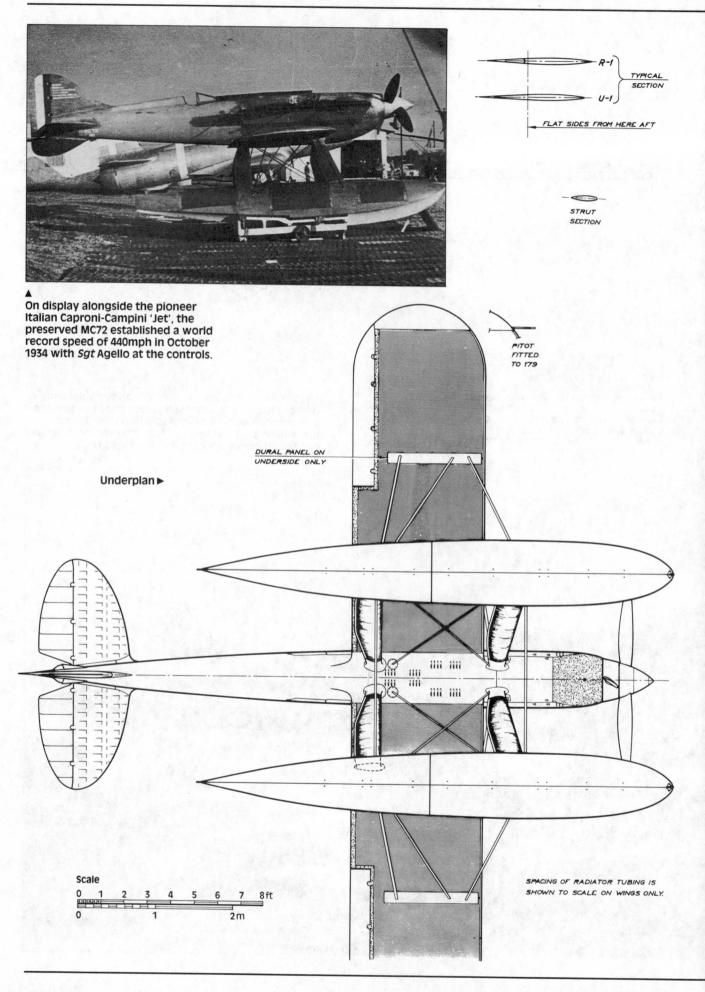

R-1 } TYPICAL SECTION
U-1

← FLAT SIDES FROM HERE AFT

STRUT SECTION

On display alongside the pioneer Italian Caproni-Campini 'Jet', the preserved MC72 established a world record speed of 440mph in October 1934 with *Sgt* Agello at the controls.

PITOT FITTED TO 179

DURAL PANEL ON UNDERSIDE ONLY

Underplan ▶

Scale

0 1 2 3 4 5 6 7 8ft
0 1 2m

SPACING OF RADIATOR TUBING IS SHOWN TO SCALE ON WINGS ONLY.

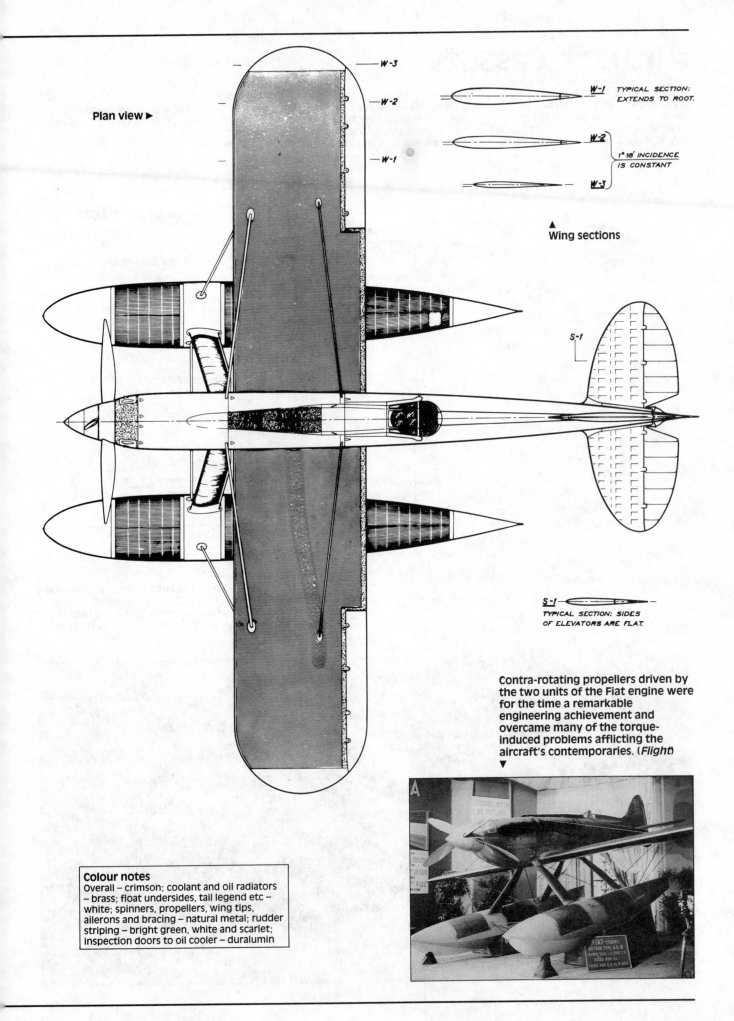

Plan view ▶

W-3

W-2

W-1

W-1   TYPICAL SECTION:
EXTENDS TO ROOT.

W-2

1° 18' INCIDENCE
IS CONSTANT

W-3

▲ Wing sections

S-1

S-1   TYPICAL SECTION: SIDES
OF ELEVATORS ARE FLAT.

Contra-rotating propellers driven by
the two units of the Fiat engine were
for the time a remarkable
engineering achievement and
overcame many of the torque-
induced problems afflicting the
aircraft's contemporaries. (*Flight*)
▼

Colour notes
Overall – crimson; coolant and oil radiators
– brass; float undersides, tail legend etc –
white; spinners, propellers, wing tips,
ailerons and bracing – natural metal; rudder
striping – bright green, white and scarlet;
inspection doors to oil cooler – duralumin

Airmark Cassutt

Country of origin: USA.
Type: Single-seat Formula One racing aircraft. Many variants constructed from original design as Cassutt Specials.
Powerplant: One Continental C-85-8F 4-cylinder engine rated at 115hp.
Dimensions: Wing span 14ft 11in *4.55m*; length 16ft 6in *5.03m*; height 4ft 3in *1.30m*; wing area 67.5 sq ft *6.3m²*.
Weights: Empty 516lb *234kg*; loaded 730lb *331kg*.
Performance: Maximum speed 230mph *370kph*; climb rate 2000ft/min *610/min*; endurance 3hr.
First flight: 1954.

DRAWN BY A A P LLOYD

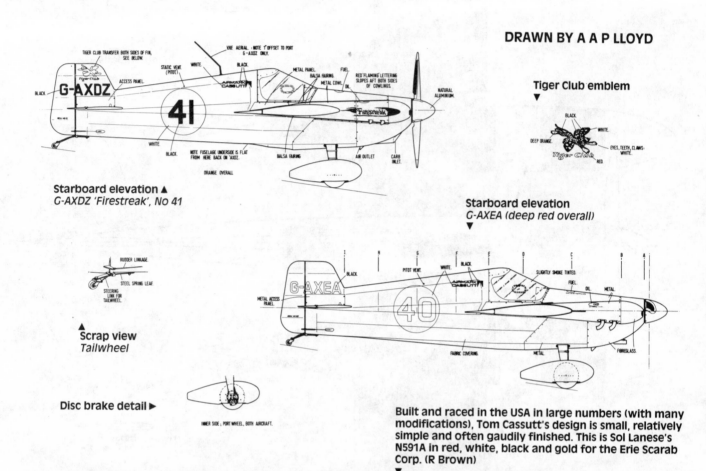

Starboard elevation ▲
G-AXDZ 'Firestreak', No 41

Tiger Club emblem
▼

Starboard elevation
G-AXEA (deep red overall)
▼

▲
Scrap view
Tailwheel

Disc brake detail ▶

Built and raced in the USA in large numbers (with many modifications), Tom Cassutt's design is small, relatively simple and often gaudily finished. This is Sol Lanese's N591A in red, white, black and gold for the Erie Scarab Corp. (R Brown)
▼

▲ Jim Clements in Jim Southworth's Cassutt 'Maybee's Baby' with its dazzling chequerboard effect. (R Brown)

A-A B-B C-C D-D E-E F-F G-G H-H I-I

Starboard elevation ▼
Showing structure

Fuselage cross-sections ►
Note that G-AXDZ has flat underside from E–E to sternpost

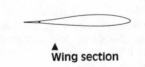

▲ **Wing section**

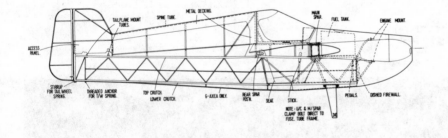

Scale

0 1 2 3 4 5 6 7 8 ft

0   1   2 m

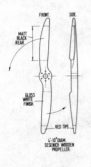

▲ **Propeller**

Front elevation ▼
G-AXDZ

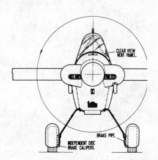

Front elevation ▼
G-AXEA

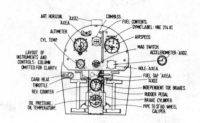

▲ **Cockpit detail**

▲
Cockpit of 'Boo Ray', a winning Cassutt in the USA, raced as
No 81 and flown by Marion Baker. (R Brown)

Scrap view▼
Starboard tailplane

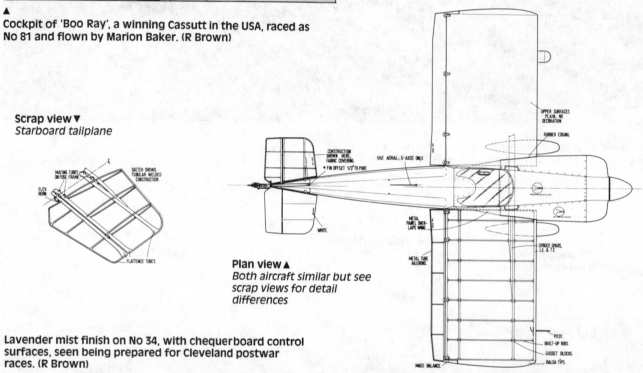

Plan view▲
*Both aircraft similar but see
scrap views for detail
differences*

Lavender mist finish on No 34, with chequerboard control
surfaces, seen being prepared for Cleveland postwar
races. (R Brown)
▼

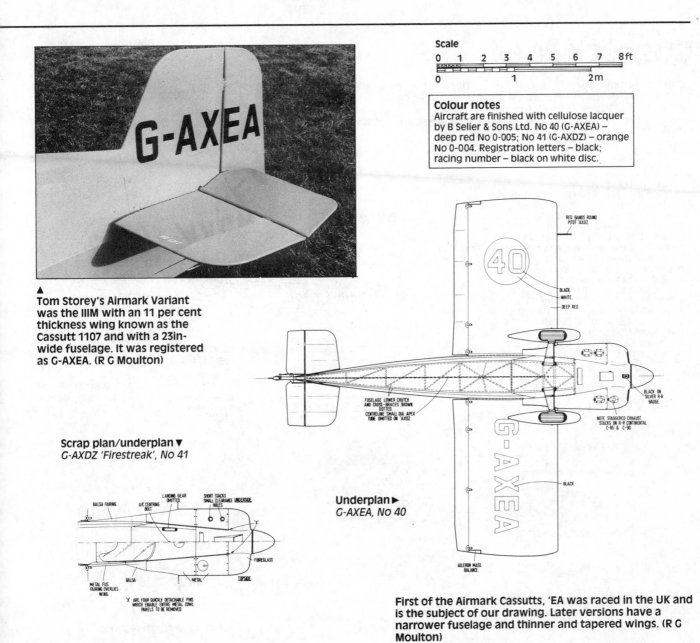

Scale

0 1 2 3 4 5 6 7 8 ft

0 1 2m

Colour notes
Aircraft are finished with cellulose lacquer by B Selier & Sons Ltd. No 40 (G-AXEA) – deep red No 0-005; No 41 (G-AXDZ) – orange No 0-004. Registration letters – black; racing number – black on white disc.

RED BANDS ROUND PITOT 'AXDZ.

40

BLACK.
WHITE.
DEEP RED.

BLACK ON
SILVER R-R
BADGE

NOTE STAGGERED EXHAUST
STACKS ON R-R CONTINENTAL
C-95 & C-90.

FUSELAGE LOWER CRUTCH
AND CROSS-BRACES SHOWN
DOTTED.
CENTRELINE SMALL DIA. APEX
TUBE OMITTED ON 'AXDZ.

G-AXEA

BLACK.

AILERON MASS
BALANCE.

▲ Tom Storey's Airmark Variant was the IIIM with an 11 per cent thickness wing known as the Cassutt 1107 and with a 23in-wide fuselage. It was registered as G-AXEA. (R G Moulton)

Scrap plan/underplan ▼
G-AXDZ 'Firestreak', No 41

BALSA FAIRING
U/C CENTRING BOLT
LANDING GEAR OMITTED.
SHORT STACKS
SMALL CLEARANCE UNDERSIDE.
HOLES.

FIBREGLASS

METAL FUS.
FAIRING OVERLIES
WING.

BALSA

METAL

TOPSIDE.

'Y' ARE FOUR QUICKLY DETACHABLE PINS
WHICH ENABLE ENTIRE METAL COWL
PANELS TO BE REMOVED.

Underplan ►
G-AXEA, No 40

First of the Airmark Cassutts, 'EA was raced in the UK and is the subject of our drawing. Later versions have a narrower fuselage and thinner and tapered wings. (R G Moulton)
▼

Chester Jeep

Country of origin: USA.
Type: Single-seat racing aircraft.
Powerplant: (Post 1936) One Menasco C4-S rated at 200hp.

Dimensions: Wing span 16ft 8in *5.08m*; length 15ft 0in *4.57m*; wing area 48 sq ft *4.5m²*.
Weights: Empty 765lb *347kg*; loaded 1150lb *522kg*.
Performance: Maximum speed 255mph *411kph*; range 325 miles *523km*.
First flight: 1932.

Colour notes

In 1935 fuselage, tail surfaces, all struts and spat stripes were dark green, and wings, fuselage stripe and spats light cream. From 1936 fuselage was cream, with green striping, and struts and tail surfaces were cream. In 1935 all numbers and lettering on fuselage and rudder were gold with black outline, except licence number and 'Art Chester' which were plain gold. Word 'Special' was in same position on starboard side with 'Chester' offset a similar distance aft instead of forward. Licence numbers were black and in late 1936 the prefix 'N' was deleted; on the rudder this was done by adding a small patch of fabric, to the outline shown.

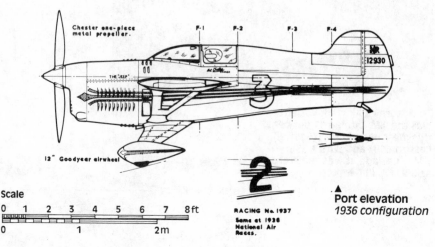

Scale

```
0  1  2  3  4  5  6  7  8 ft
0          1          2m
```

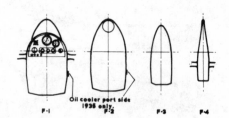

▲ **Port elevation**
1936 configuration

Port elevation ▼
1935 configuration

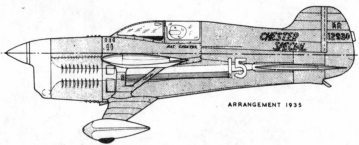

▲ **Fuselage cross-sections**

Art Chester in the Jeep at the National Air Races in 1936 – the first year of its familiar cream and green decoration. Top speed in these races was 230mph.
▼

▲
The wing plan of the ultimate Jeep is best seen in Dan Clutz's perfect model, a 2nd place winner at the 1959 US Nats.

▲
At Oakland in 1938 for the Pacific Air Races, the Jeep was becoming outclassed by the new breed of refined and better-powered competitors.

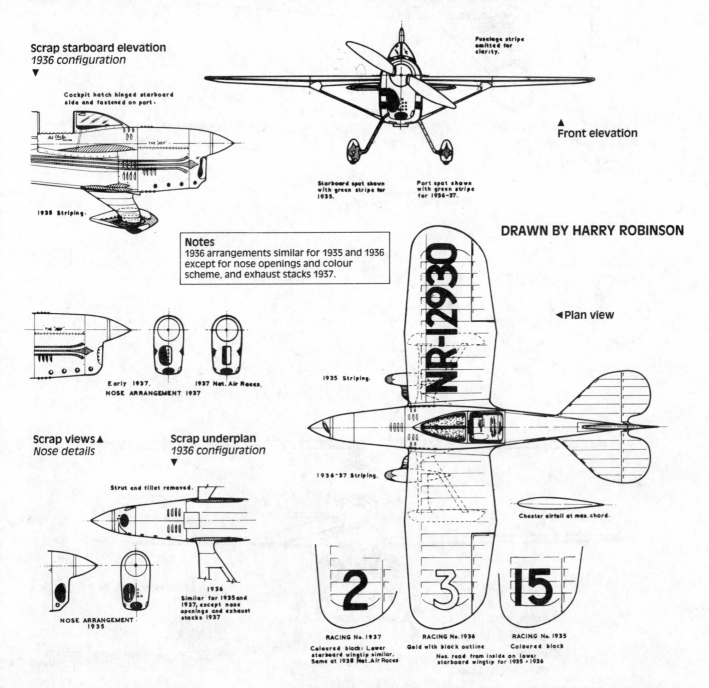

Scrap starboard elevation
1936 configuration
▼

Cockpit hatch hinged starboard side and fastened on port.

THE JEEP

1935 Striping.

Fuselage stripe omitted for clarity.

▲
Front elevation

Starboard spat shown with green stripe for 1935.

Port spat shown with green stripe for 1936-37.

Notes
1936 arrangements similar for 1935 and 1936 except for nose openings and colour scheme, and exhaust stacks 1937.

DRAWN BY HARRY ROBINSON

THE JEEP

Early 1937.

1937 Nat. Air Races.

NOSE ARRANGEMENT 1937

NR-12930

1935 Striping.

1936-37 Striping.

◄**Plan view**

Chester airfoil at max. chord.

Scrap views▲
Nose details

Scrap underplan
1936 configuration
▼

Strut and fillet removed.

1936
Similar for 1935 and 1937, except nose openings and exhaust stacks 1937

NOSE ARRANGEMENT 1935

2

RACING No. 1937
Coloured black: Lower starboard wingtip similar. Same at 1938 Nat. Air Races

3

RACING No. 1936
Gold with black outline

Nos. read from inside on lower starboard wingtip for 1935 / 1936

15

RACING No. 1935
Coloured black

Curtiss CR-1, 2 and 3

Country of origin: USA.
Type: Single-seat racing aircraft.
Powerplant: One Curtiss D12 twelve-cylinder engine rated at 400hp, (CR-3) 450hp.
Dimensions: Wing span 22ft 8in *6.91m*; length 21ft 0in *6.40m*, (CR-3) 25ft 0½in

7.63m; wing area 168 sq ft *15.6m²*.
Weights: Empty 1665lb *755kg*, (CR-2) 1782lb *808kg*, (CR-3) 2119lb *961kg*; loaded 2095lb *950kg*, (CR-2) 2212lb *1003kg*, (CR-3) 2746lb *1246kg*.
Performance: Maximum speed about 185mph *298kph*, (CR-3) 193mph *311kph*;

climb to 14,300ft *4360m* 10min; service ceiling 24,000ft *7315m*, (CR-3) 22,000ft *6700m*.
First flight: August 1921, (CR-2) 1922, (CR-3) 1923.

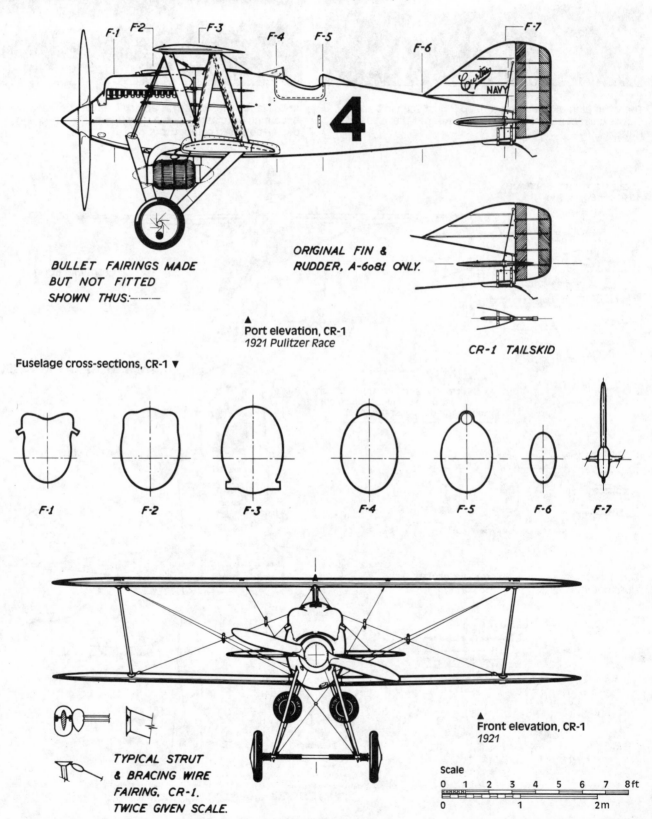

BULLET FAIRINGS MADE
BUT NOT FITTED
SHOWN THUS:———

ORIGINAL FIN &
RUDDER, A-6081 ONLY.

▲ Port elevation, CR-1
1921 Pulitzer Race

CR-1 TAILSKID

Fuselage cross-sections, CR-1 ▼

F-1 F-2 F-3 F-4 F-5 F-6 F-7

TYPICAL STRUT
& BRACING WIRE
FAIRING, CR-1.
TWICE GIVEN SCALE.

▲ Front elevation, CR-1
1921

Scale
0 1 2 3 4 5 6 7 8ft
0 1 2m

Plan view, CR-1 ▲

▲ Developed from the drawn CR-3 was this equally small R2C-1 first flown by Lt Harold Brow in September 1923. It recorded 244.3mph within four days – the first aircraft to fly at four miles a minute!

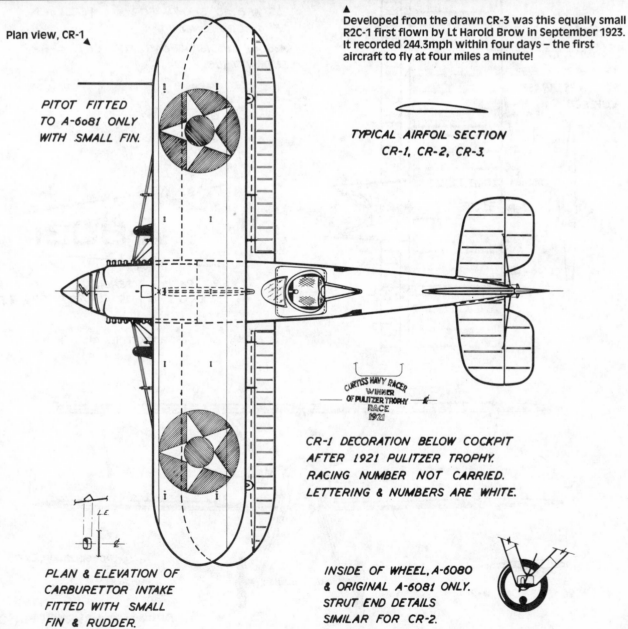

PITOT FITTED
TO A-6081 ONLY
WITH SMALL FIN.

TYPICAL AIRFOIL SECTION
CR-1, CR-2, CR-3.

CURTISS NAVY RACER
WINNER
OF PULITZER TROPHY
RACE
1921

CR-1 DECORATION BELOW COCKPIT
AFTER 1921 PULITZER TROPHY.
RACING NUMBER NOT CARRIED.
LETTERING & NUMBERS ARE WHITE.

PLAN & ELEVATION OF
CARBURETTOR INTAKE
FITTED WITH SMALL
FIN & RUDDER.

INSIDE OF WHEEL, A-6080
& ORIGINAL A-6081 ONLY.
STRUT END DETAILS
SIMILAR FOR CR-2.

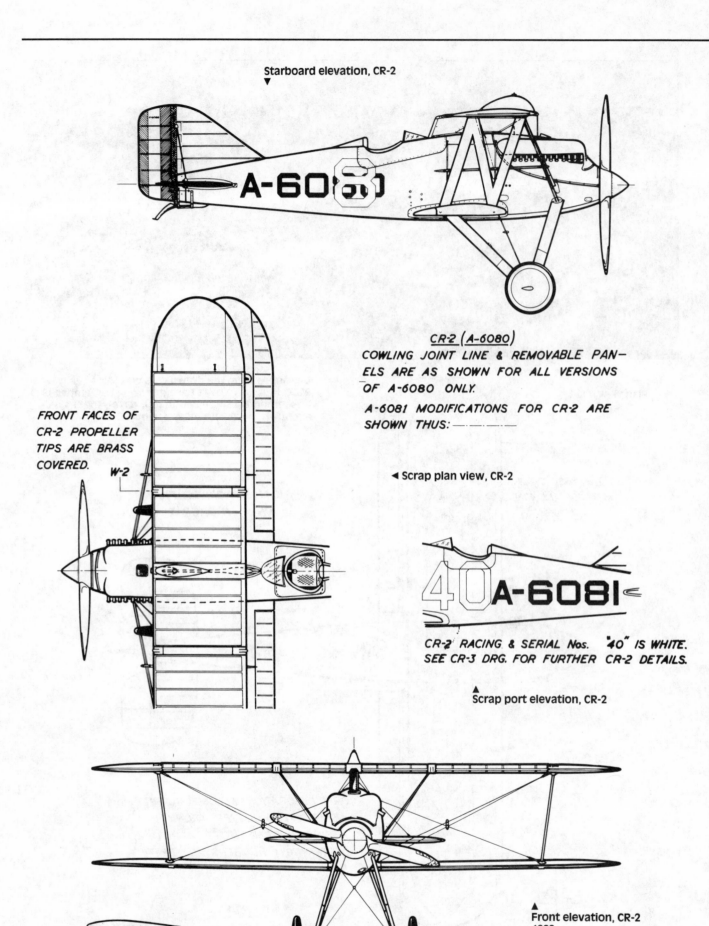

Starboard elevation, CR-2

A-6080

FRONT FACES OF
CR-2 PROPELLER
TIPS ARE BRASS
COVERED.

W-2

CR-2 (A-6080)
COWLING JOINT LINE & REMOVABLE PAN—
ELS ARE AS SHOWN FOR ALL VERSIONS
OF A-6080 ONLY.

A-6081 MODIFICATIONS FOR CR-2 ARE
SHOWN THUS: ———————

◄ Scrap plan view, CR-2

40 A-6081

CR-2 RACING & SERIAL Nos. "40" IS WHITE.
SEE CR-3 DRG. FOR FURTHER CR-2 DETAILS.

▲ Scrap port elevation, CR-2

▲ Front elevation, CR-2
1922

WING SECTION W-2

DRAWN BY HARRY ROBINSON

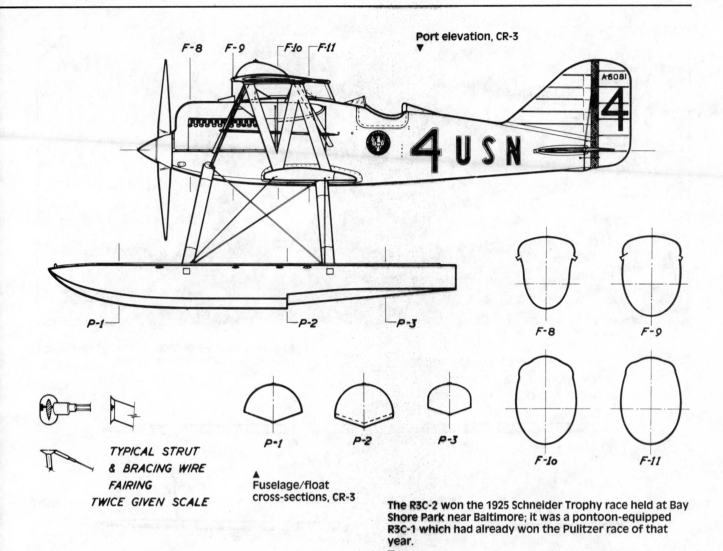

Port elevation, CR-3

F-8 F-9 F-10 F-11

A-6081

4 USN

4

P-1 P-2 P-3

F-8 F-9

F-10 F-11

TYPICAL STRUT
& BRACING WIRE
FAIRING
TWICE GIVEN SCALE

P-1 P-2 P-3

▲ Fuselage/float
cross-sections, CR-3

The R3C-2 won the 1925 Schneider Trophy race held at Bay
Shore Park near Baltimore; it was a pontoon-equipped
R3C-1 which had already won the Pulitzer race of that
year.
▼

As drawn, the CR-3 (A-6080), a sister of 6081 which won the 1923 Schneider at 188mph.

RUDDER HINGE LINES ARE FAIRED WITH HEAVILY DOPED FABRIC. COLOUR IS DEEP AMBER-RED.

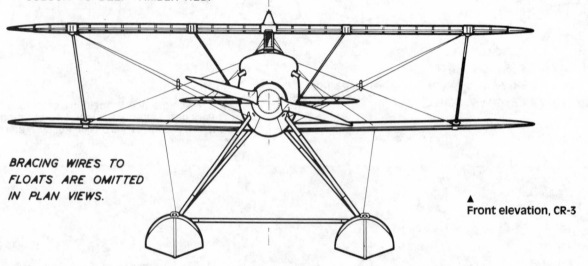

BRACING WIRES TO FLOATS ARE OMITTED IN PLAN VIEWS.

Front elevation, CR-3

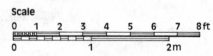

Scale
0 1 2 3 4 5 6 7 8ft
0   1   2m

◄ Restored and displayed at the NAM (Smithsonian), Washington, DC, is the last of the Curtiss seaplane racers – the R3C-2 which won the 1925 Schneider Trophy at 232mph with James H Doolittle at the controls. (R G Moulton)

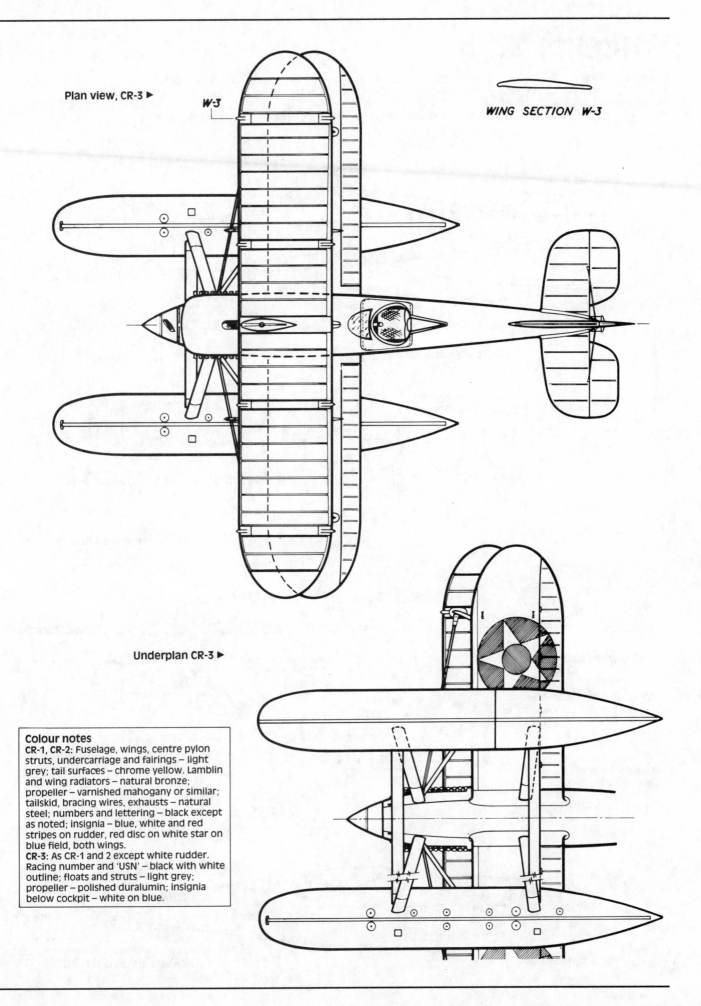

Plan view, CR-3 ▶

W-3

WING SECTION W-3

Underplan CR-3 ▶

Colour notes

CR-1, CR-2: Fuselage, wings, centre pylon struts, undercarriage and fairings – light grey; tail surfaces – chrome yellow. Lamblin and wing radiators – natural bronze; propeller – varnished mahogany or similar; tailskid, bracing wires, exhausts – natural steel; numbers and lettering – black except as noted; insignia – blue, white and red stripes on rudder, red disc on white star on blue field, both wings.

CR-3: As CR-1 and 2 except white rudder. Racing number and 'USN' – black with white outline; floats and struts – light grey; propeller – polished duralumin; insignia below cockpit – white on blue.

Folkerts SK-3

Country of origin: USA.
Type: Single-seat racing aircraft.
Powerplant: One Menasco Super
Buccaneer C65-4 engine rated at 400hp.

Dimensions: Wing span 16ft 4in *4.98m*;
length 22ft 0in *6.71m*; wing area 55 sq ft
5.1m².
Weights: Empty 841lb *381kg*; loaded

1385lb *628kg*.
Performance: Maximum speed 305–
308mph *491–496kph*.
First flight: 1937.

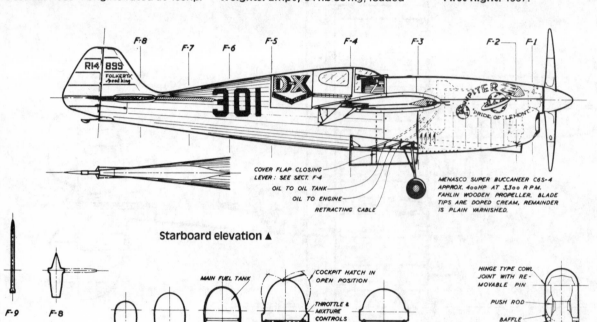

COVER FLAP CLOSING
LEVER : SEE SECT. F-4
OIL TO OIL TANK
OIL TO ENGINE
RETRACTING CABLE

MENASCO SUPER BUCCANEER C65-4
APPROX. 400HP AT 3,300 R.P.M.
FAHLIN WOODEN PROPELLER. BLADE
TIPS ARE DOPED CREAM, REMAINDER
IS PLAIN VARNISHED.

Starboard elevation ▲

F-9 F-8 F-7 F-6

MAIN FUEL TANK

AUX'L'Y
TANK
F-5

CANVAS
SEAT

COCKPIT HATCH IN
OPEN POSITION

THROTTLE &
MIXTURE
CONTROLS

SEE PORT
ELEVATION
FOR TRUE
LOCATION

F-4

SHOCK CORD

AIR EXIT

AXES OF MAIN &
SECONDARY TRUSSES

F-3

HINGE TYPE COWL
JOINT WITH RE-
MOVABLE PIN

PUSH ROD

BAFFLE

INTAKE
MANIFOLD

CARBURETTOR
INTAKE
F-2

EXHAUST

F-1

▲ Fuselage cross-sections

ALCLAD COVER   RETAINING STRAP

COLUMN
FULL FOR'D

TO ELEVATORS

TO ENGINE   TO RUDDER

◄ Scrap views
Cockpit details

OIL TEMP.
IGNITION
SWITCH
TACHOMETER
CYLINDER HEAD TEMP.
AIRSPEED
INDICATOR
MANIFOLD
PRESSURE
PLYWOOD

INSTRUMENT PANEL: TWICE GIVEN SCALE

Instrument panel ►
Twice given scale

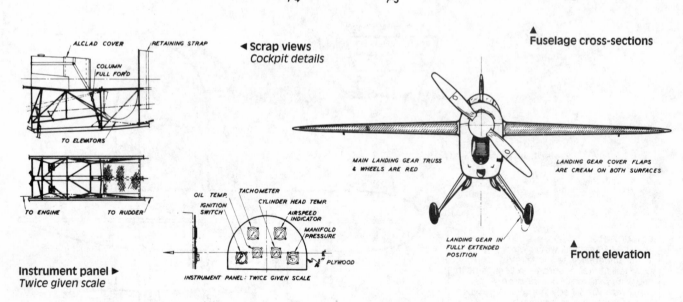

MAIN LANDING GEAR TRUSS
& WHEELS ARE RED

LANDING GEAR COVER FLAPS
ARE CREAM ON BOTH SURFACES

LANDING GEAR IN
FULLY EXTENDED
POSITION

▲ Front elevation

Port elevation
▼

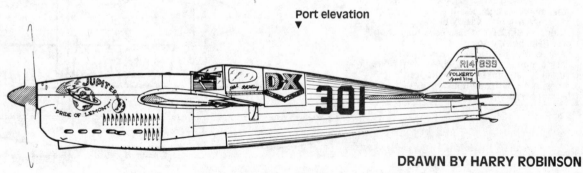

DRAWN BY HARRY ROBINSON

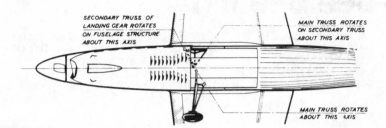

SECONDARY TRUSS OF LANDING GEAR ROTATES ON FUSELAGE STRUCTURE ABOUT THIS AXIS

MAIN TRUSS ROTATES ON SECONDARY TRUSS ABOUT THIS AXIS

MAIN TRUSS ROTATES ABOUT THIS AXIS

Colour notes
Entire aircraft – yellow-cream.
Cowling insignia: 'Jupiter', front of comet, fiery tails and 'Pride of Lemont' – red; rear of comet – white; halo to Jupiter – white with black edge; lettering on cockpit hatch – red; 'D-X' – red with black edge and black chevron and white lettering.

NOTE THAT IN THE INVERTED PLAN & SECTION F3 THE MAIN TRUSS ONLY IS DRAWN ON THE STARBOARD SIDE OF THE AIRCRAFT, IN OUTLINE ONLY, & THE SECONDARY TRUSS ONLY IS DRAWN ON THE PORT SIDE IN SOLID LINES.

IN THE PORT ELEVATION THE MAIN TRUSS IS ALSO SHOWN IN OUTLINE & THE SECONDARY TRUSS IN SOLID LINES.

LANDING GEAR COVER FLAPS ARE OMITTED IN INVERTED PLAN

— WT

Plan view ▶

WING SECTION WT. NACA 2406 SECTION BETWEEN WT & TIP IS NACA 2406 WITH SHARPENED LEADING EDGE.

— HINGE

WING SECTION AT ROOT. NACA 2409

— HINGE

▲ **Scrap underplan**

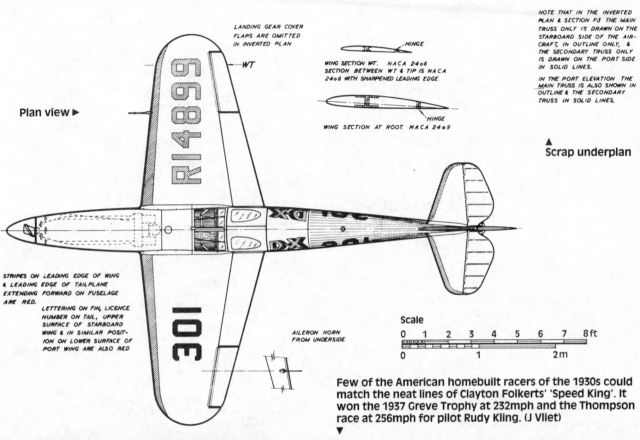

STRIPES ON LEADING EDGE OF WING & LEADING EDGE OF TAILPLANE EXTENDING FORWARD ON FUSELAGE ARE RED.

LETTERING ON FIN, LICENCE NUMBER ON TAIL, UPPER SURFACE OF STARBOARD WING & IN SIMILAR POSITION ON LOWER SURFACE OF PORT WING ARE ALSO RED

AILERON HORN FROM UNDERSIDE

Scale

0 1 2 3 4 5 6 7 8 ft

0 1 2m

Few of the American homebuilt racers of the 1930s could match the neat lines of Clayton Folkerts' 'Speed King'. It won the 1937 Greve Trophy at 232mph and the Thompson race at 256mph for pilot Rudy Kling. (J Vliet)
▼

Gee Bee R-1

Country of origin: USA.
Type: Single-seat racing aircraft.
Powerplant: One Pratt & Whitney Wasp radial engine rated at 730hp.
Dimensions: Wing span 25ft 0in *7.62m;*

length 17ft 0in *5.18m,* (with Hamilton Standard propeller) 18ft 4½in *5.60m,* (in 1933) about 18ft 10in *5.74m;* wing area 100 sq ft *9.29m².*
Weights: Empty 1840lb *834kg;* loaded

3075lb *1395kg.*
Performance: Maximum speed 309mph *497kph.*
First flight: 13 August 1932

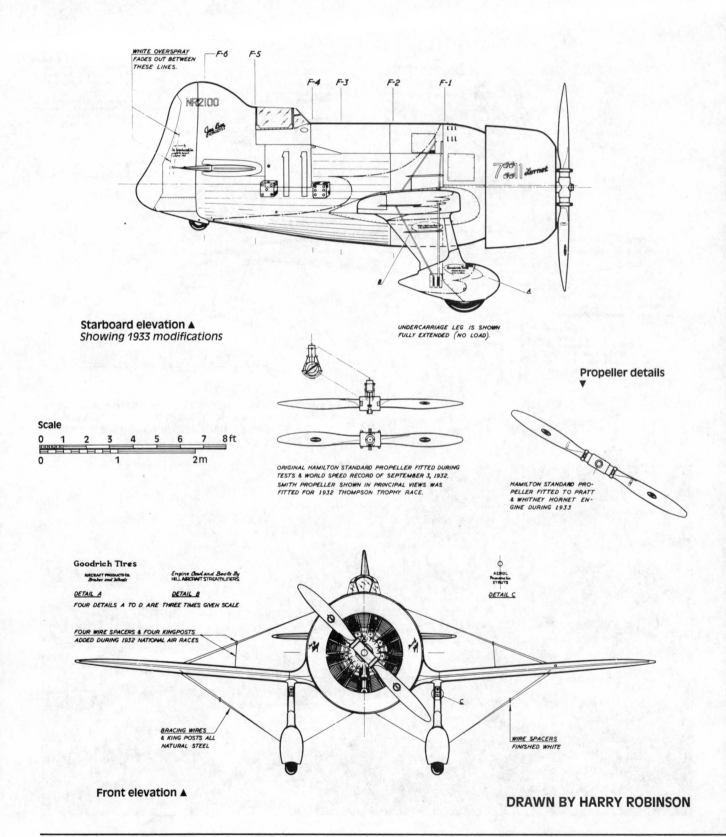

Starboard elevation ▲
Showing 1933 modifications

UNDERCARRIAGE LEG IS SHOWN
FULLY EXTENDED (NO LOAD).

Propeller details
▼

Scale
0 1 2 3 4 5 6 7 8ft
0 1 2m

ORIGINAL HAMILTON STANDARD PROPELLER FITTED DURING
TESTS & WORLD SPEED RECORD OF SEPTEMBER 3, 1932.
SMITH PROPELLER SHOWN IN PRINCIPAL VIEWS WAS
FITTED FOR 1932 THOMPSON TROPHY RACE.

HAMILTON STANDARD PRO-
PELLER FITTED TO PRATT
& WHITNEY HORNET EN-
GINE DURING 1933

Goodrich Tires

AIRCRAFT PRODUCTS CO.
Brakes and Wheels

Engine Cowl and Boots By
HILL AIRCRAFT STREAMLINERS

AEROL
Pneumatic
STRUTS

DETAIL A   DETAIL B   DETAIL C

FOUR DETAILS A TO D ARE THREE TIMES GIVEN SCALE

FOUR WIRE SPACERS & FOUR KINGPOSTS
ADDED DURING 1932 NATIONAL AIR RACES

BRACING WIRES
& KING POSTS ALL
NATURAL STEEL

WIRE SPACERS
FINISHED WHITE

Front elevation ▲

DRAWN BY HARRY ROBINSON

The 1932 standard Gee Bee R-1, first in the Thompson Trophy for James Doolittle at 252mph. ▶

Note
Plan view and port and front elevations show R-1 as flown in the 1932 Thompson Trophy Race. 1933 modifications comprised added rudder area, non-castoring tailwheel and larger propeller and engine cowling. Centreline of engine was approx ¾in below fuselage datum.

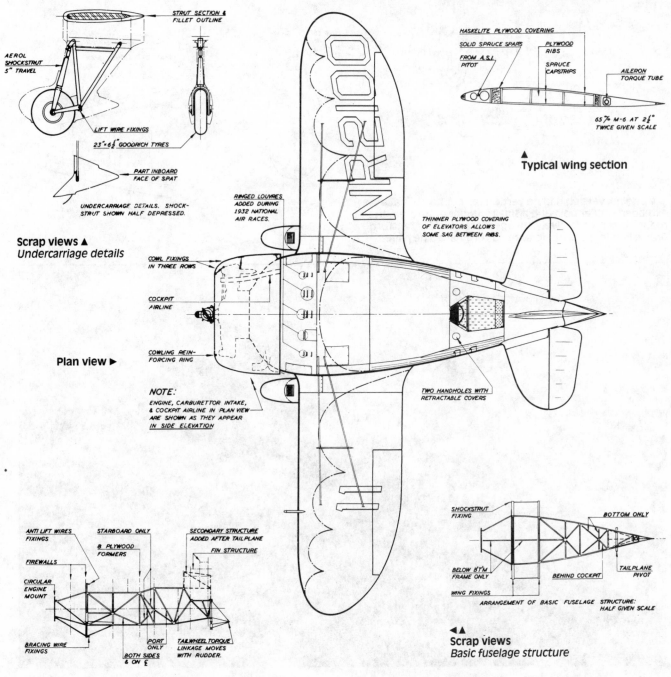

STRUT SECTION & FILLET OUTLINE

AEROL SHOCKSTRUT 5" TRAVEL

LIFT WIRE FIXINGS

23"×6½" GOODRICH TYRES

PART INBOARD FACE OF SPAT

UNDERCARRIAGE DETAILS. SHOCK-STRUT SHOWN HALF DEPRESSED.

Scrap views ▲
Undercarriage details

HASKELITE PLYWOOD COVERING
SOLID SPRUCE SPARS
PLYWOOD RIBS
FROM A.S.I. PITOT
SPRUCE CAPSTRIPS
AILERON TORQUE TUBE

65% M-6 AT 2½°
TWICE GIVEN SCALE

▲ Typical wing section

RINGED LOUVRES ADDED DURING 1932 NATIONAL AIR RACES.

THINNER PLYWOOD COVERING OF ELEVATORS ALLOWS SOME SAG BETWEEN RIBS.

COWL FIXINGS IN THREE ROWS

COCKPIT AIRLINE

Plan view ▶

COWLING REIN-FORCING RING

TWO HANDHOLES WITH RETRACTABLE COVERS

NOTE:
ENGINE, CARBURETTOR INTAKE, & COCKPIT AIRLINE IN PLAN VIEW ARE SHOWN AS THEY APPEAR IN SIDE ELEVATION

ANTI LIFT WIRES FIXINGS
STARBOARD ONLY
SECONDARY STRUCTURE ADDED AFTER TAILPLANE
8 PLYWOOD FORMERS
FIN STRUCTURE
FIREWALLS
CIRCULAR ENGINE MOUNT
BRACING WIRE FIXINGS
PORT ONLY
BOTH SIDES & ON ₵
TAILWHEEL TORQUE LINKAGE MOVES WITH RUDDER.

SHOCKSTRUT FIXING
BOTTOM ONLY
BELOW B'T'M FRAME ONLY
BEHIND COCKPIT
TAILPLANE PIVOT
WING FIXINGS
ARRANGEMENT OF BASIC FUSELAGE STRUCTURE: HALF GIVEN SCALE

◀▲ Scrap views
Basic fuselage structure

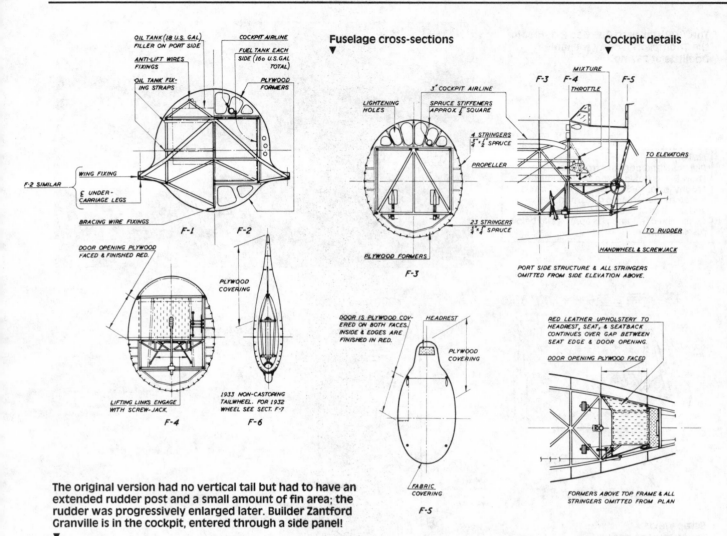

Fuselage cross-sections ▼

Cockpit details ▼

OIL TANK (18 U.S. GAL) FILLER ON PORT SIDE

COCKPIT AIRLINE

FUEL TANK EACH SIDE (160 U.S. GAL TOTAL)

ANTI-LIFT WIRES FIXINGS

OIL TANK FIX-ING STRAPS

PLYWOOD FORMERS

F-2 SIMILAR

WING FIXING

€ UNDER-CARRIAGE LEGS

BRACING WIRE FIXINGS

F-1

F-2

LIGHTENING HOLES

3" COCKPIT AIRLINE

SPRUCE STIFFENERS APPROX ¼" SQUARE

4 STRINGERS ⅝" × ½" SPRUCE

PROPELLER

23 STRINGERS ¾" × ¼" SPRUCE

PLYWOOD FORMERS

F-3

F-3   F-4   F-5

MIXTURE

THROTTLE

TO ELEVATORS

TO RUDDER

HANDWHEEL & SCREWJACK

PORT SIDE STRUCTURE & ALL STRINGERS OMITTED FROM SIDE ELEVATION ABOVE.

DOOR OPENING PLYWOOD FACED & FINISHED RED.

PLYWOOD COVERING

LIFTING LINKS ENGAGE WITH SCREW-JACK.

F-4

1933 NON-CASTORING TAILWHEEL. FOR 1932 WHEEL SEE SECT. F-7

F-6

DOOR IS PLYWOOD COV-ERED ON BOTH FACES. INSIDE & EDGES ARE FINISHED IN RED.

HEADREST

PLYWOOD COVERING

FABRIC COVERING

F-5

RED LEATHER UPHOLSTERY TO HEADREST, SEAT, & SEATBACK CONTINUES OVER GAP BETWEEN SEAT EDGE & DOOR OPENING.

DOOR OPENING PLYWOOD FACED

FORMERS ABOVE TOP FRAME & ALL STRINGERS OMITTED FROM PLAN

The original version had no vertical tail but had to have an extended rudder post and a small amount of fin area; the rudder was progressively enlarged later. Builder Zantford Granville is in the cockpit, entered through a side panel!
▼

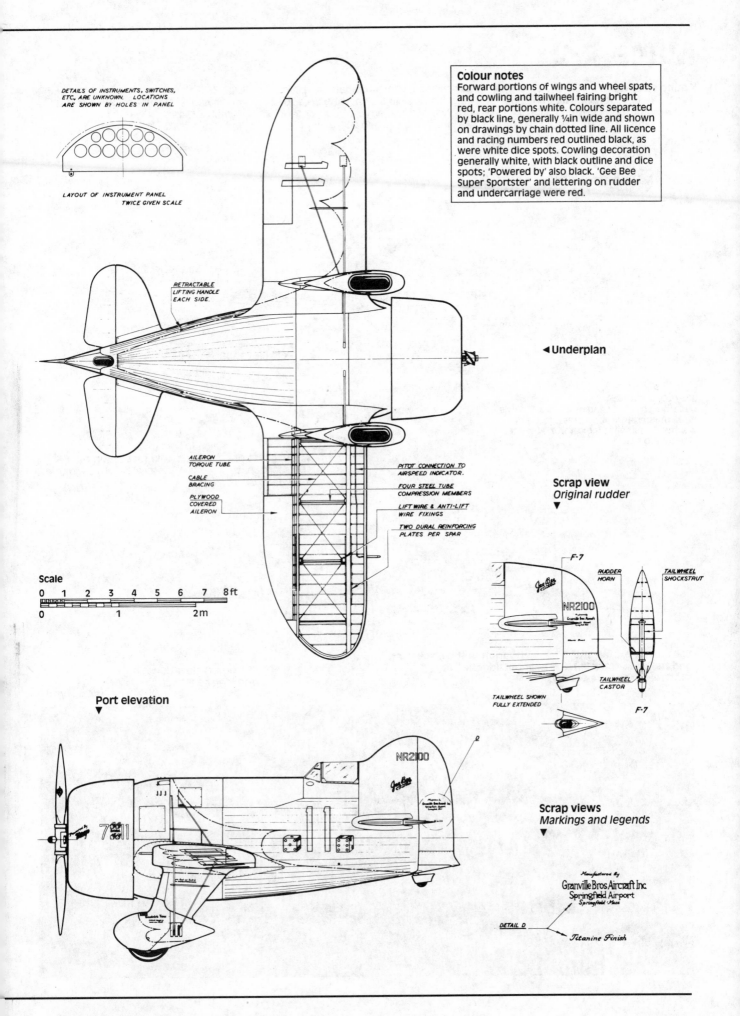

DETAILS OF INSTRUMENTS, SWITCHES, ETC., ARE UNKNOWN. LOCATIONS ARE SHOWN BY HOLES IN PANEL

LAYOUT OF INSTRUMENT PANEL
TWICE GIVEN SCALE

Colour notes

Forward portions of wings and wheel spats, and cowling and tailwheel fairing bright red, rear portions white. Colours separated by black line, generally ¼in wide and shown on drawings by chain dotted line. All licence and racing numbers red outlined black, as were white dice spots. Cowling decoration generally white, with black outline and dice spots; 'Powered by' also black. 'Gee Bee Super Sportster' and lettering on rudder and undercarriage were red.

RETRACTABLE LIFTING HANDLE EACH SIDE.

◄ Underplan

AILERON TORQUE TUBE

CABLE BRACING

PLYWOOD COVERED AILERON

PITOT CONNECTION TO AIRSPEED INDICATOR.

FOUR STEEL TUBE COMPRESSION MEMBERS

LIFT WIRE & ANTI-LIFT WIRE FIXINGS

TWO DURAL REINFORCING PLATES PER SPAR

Scrap view
Original rudder
▼

F-7

RUDDER HORN

TAILWHEEL SHOCKSTRUT

NR2100

TAILWHEEL CASTOR

TAILWHEEL SHOWN FULLY EXTENDED

F-7

Scale

```
0  1  2  3  4  5  6  7   8 ft
0           1           2m
```

Port elevation
▼

NR2100

Scrap views
Markings and legends
▼

Manufactured By
Granville Bros Aircraft Inc.
Springfield Airport
Springfield Mass

DETAIL D

Titanine Finish

Mace R-2

Country of origin: USA.
Type: Single-seat racing aircraft.
Powerplant: One Continental 0-200-A engine rated at 100hp.

Dimensions: Wing span 16ft 0in *4.88m*; length 18ft 2¼in *5.54m*; wing area 70 sq ft *6.50m²*.
Weights: Empty 540lb *245kg*; loaded

800lb *363kg*.
Performance: Maximum speed about 200mph *322kph*.
First flight: 1970.

DRAWN BY A A P LLOYD

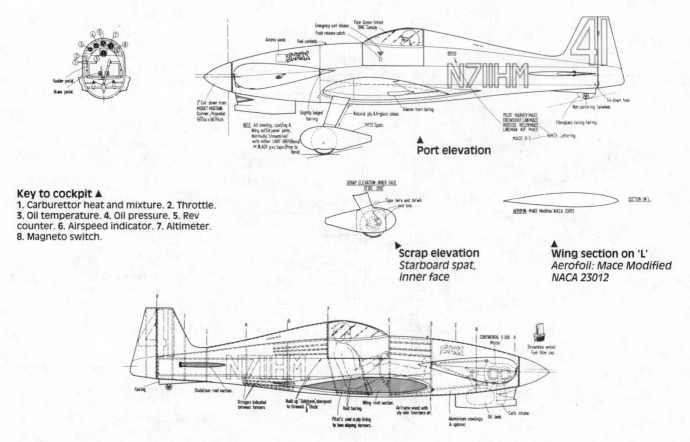

▲ **Port elevation**

Scrap elevation
Starboard spat, inner face

Wing section on 'L'
Aerofoil: Mace Modified NACA 23012

Key to cockpit ▲
1. Carburettor heat and mixture. 2. Throttle.
3. Oil temperature. 4. Oil pressure. 5. Rev counter. 6. Airspeed indicator. 7. Altimeter.
8. Magneto switch.

▲ **Starboard elevation**
Showing construction

The curved profile of the front elevation of the Mace wing and the wide-track landing gear outside the prop slipstream are noteworthy.
▼

▲ Harvey Mace has made a succession of Formula One racers and homebuilts: this is possibly the most attractive on account of its curvaceous lines.

▲ **Fuselage cross-sections**

Scale

```
0   1   2   3   4   5   6   7   8ft
0               1               2m
```

Front elevation ▼

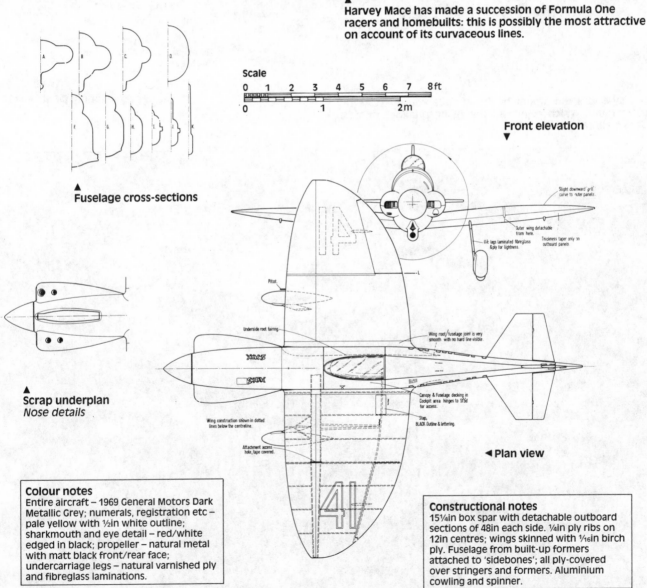

Slight downward 'grill' curve to outer panels.

Outer wing detachable from here.

U/c legs laminated fibreglass & ply for lightness.

Thickness taper only on outboard panels.

Pitot.

Underside root fairing

Wing root/fuselage joint is very smooth with no hard line visible.

Canopy & Fuselage decking in Cockpit area hinges to STBD for access.

Step, BLACK Outline & lettering.

Wing construction shown in dotted lines below the centreline.

Attachment access hole, tape covered.

◄ **Plan view**

▲ **Scrap underplan**
Nose details

Colour notes
Entire aircraft – 1969 General Motors Dark Metallic Grey; numerals, registration etc – pale yellow with ½in white outline; sharkmouth and eye detail – red/white edged in black; propeller – natural metal with matt black front/rear face; undercarriage legs – natural varnished ply and fibreglass laminations.

Constructional notes
15¼in box spar with detachable outboard sections of 48in each side. ¼in ply ribs on 12in centres; wings skinned with ¹⁄₁₆in birch ply. Fuselage from built-up formers attached to 'sidebones'; all ply-covered over stringers and formers. Aluminium cowling and spinner.

Stampe & Vertongen SV-4B and C

Country of origin: Belgium.
Type: Single- or two-seat aerobatic aircraft.
Powerplant: One De Havilland Gipsy Major III engine rated at 120hp or
Renault 4p rated at 140hp.
Dimensions: Wing span 26ft 2in *7.98m*; length 22ft 3in *6.78m*; height 8ft 6in *2.59m*; wing area 194 sq ft *18m²*.
Weights: Empty 1058lb *480kg*; loaded
1719lb *780kg*.
Performance: Maximum speed 124mph *200kph*; time to 3280ft *1000m*, 4min; absolute ceiling 19,680ft *6000m*.
First flight: 1928.

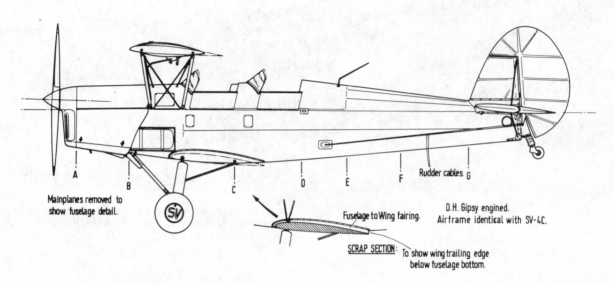

A   B   C   D   E   F   Rudder cables. G

Mainplanes removed to
show fuselage detail.

Fuselage to Wing fairing.

D.H. Gipsy engined.
Airframe identical with SV-4C.

SCRAP SECTION: To show wing trailing edge
below fuselage bottom.

▲
Port elevation, SV-4B

The SV-4 was the mount of the famous Rothmans Aerobatic Team, which displayed the flying qualities of this classic aircraft to the full.
▼

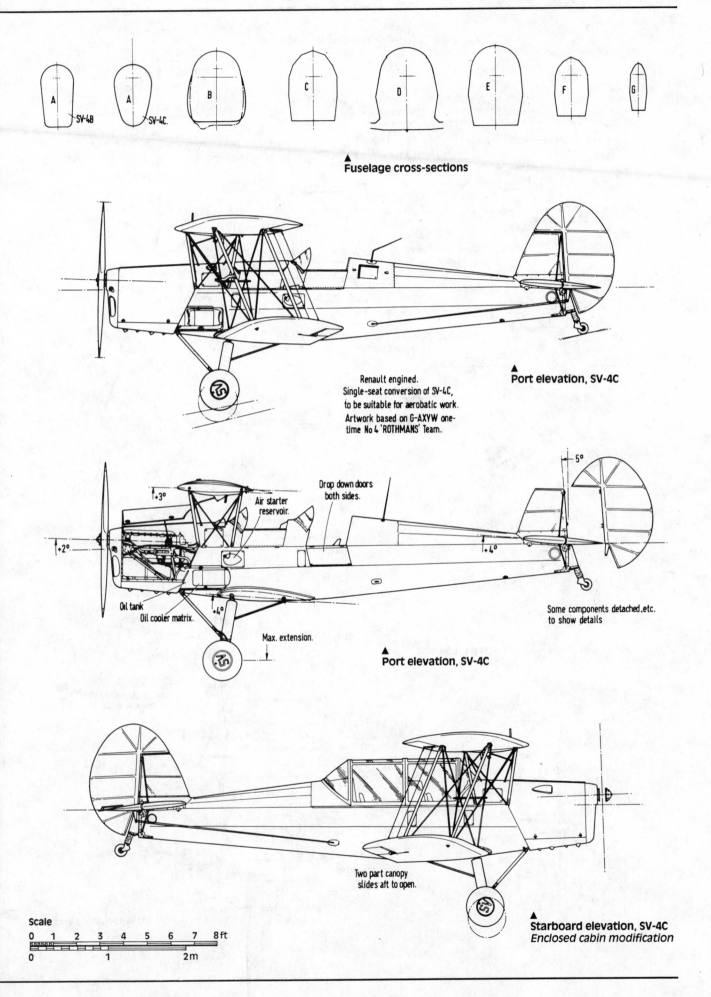

▲ Fuselage cross-sections

Renault engined.
Single-seat conversion of SV-4C,
to be suitable for aerobatic work.
Artwork based on G-AXYW one-
time No 4 'ROTHMANS' Team.

▲ Port elevation, SV-4C

Air starter
reservoir.

Drop down doors
both sides.

Oil tank

Oil cooler matrix.

Max. extension.

Some components detached, etc.
to show details

▲ Port elevation, SV-4C

Two part canopy
slides aft to open.

▲ Starboard elevation, SV-4C
Enclosed cabin modification

Scale

0 1 2 3 4 5 6 7 8 ft

0 1 2 m

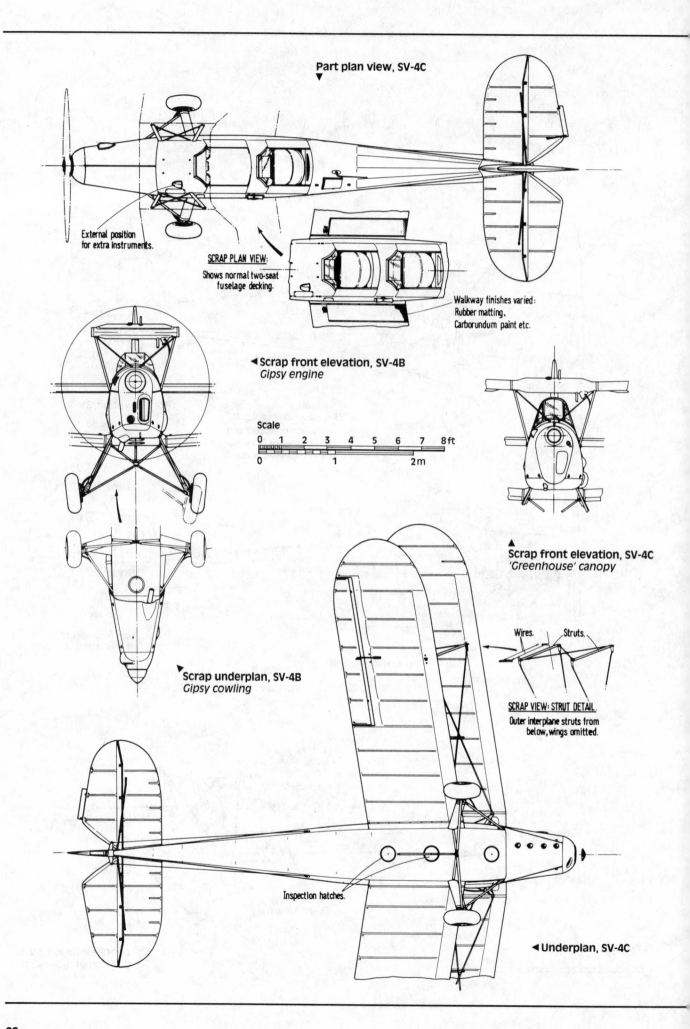

Part plan view, SV-4C

External position
for extra instruments.

SCRAP PLAN VIEW:
Shows normal two-seat
fuselage decking.

Walkway finishes varied:
Rubber matting,
Carborundum paint etc.

◄ **Scrap front elevation, SV-4B**
Gipsy engine

Scale

0 1 2 3 4 5 6 7 8 ft

0   1   2m

▲
Scrap front elevation, SV-4C
'Greenhouse' canopy

Wires.   Struts.

SCRAP VIEW: STRUT DETAIL.
Outer interplane struts from
below, wings omitted.

▼ **Scrap underplan, SV-4B**
Gipsy cowling

Inspection hatches.

◄ **Underplan, SV-4C**

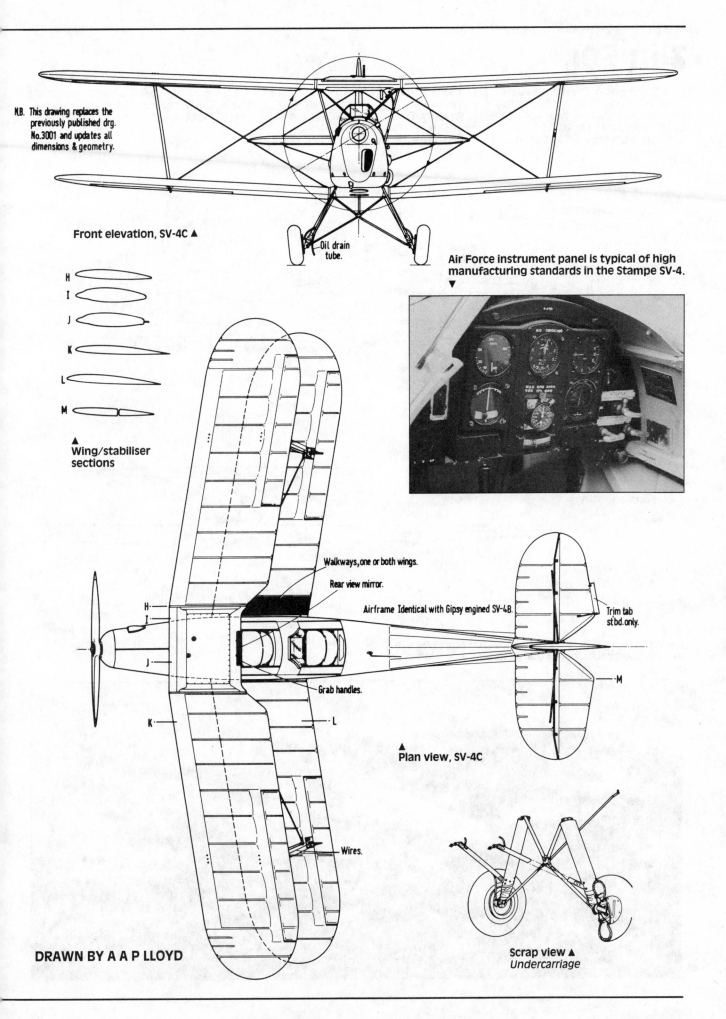

N.B. This drawing replaces the previously published drg. No.3001 and updates all dimensions & geometry.

Front elevation, SV-4C ▲

Oil drain tube.

H
I
J
K
L
M

▲ **Wing/stabiliser sections**

Air Force instrument panel is typical of high manufacturing standards in the Stampe SV-4.
▼

Walkways, one or both wings.

Rear view mirror.

Airframe Identical with Gipsy engined SV-4B.

Trim tab st'bd. only.

H
I

J

Grab handles.

K — — L

— M

Plan view, SV-4C ▲

Wires.

DRAWN BY A A P LLOYD

Scrap view ▲
Undercarriage

Zlin 50L

Country of origin: Czechoslovakia.
Type: Single-seat aerobatic aircraft.
Powerplant: One Lycoming AE10-540-04-B5 engine rated at 260hp.
Dimensions: Wing span 28ft 2½in

8.60m; length 21ft 7in *6.58m*; height 6ft 0½in *1.84m*.
Weights: Empty 1279lb *580kg*; maximum 1764lb *800kg*.
Performance: Maximum speed 175mph

282kph; climb rate 2500ft/min *760m/min*; load limits +9/−6g.
First flight: Autumn 1975

Port elevation ▼

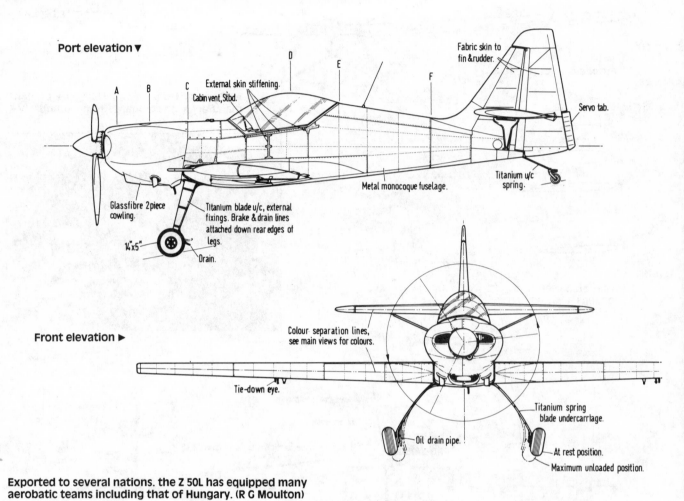

- Fabric skin to fin & rudder.
- Servo tab.
- External skin stiffening.
- Cabin vent, Stbd.
- A B C D E F
- Glassfibre 2 piece cowling.
- Titanium blade u/c, external fixings. Brake & drain lines attached down rear edges of legs.
- 14"x5"
- Drain.
- Metal monocoque fuselage.
- Titanium u/c spring.

Front elevation ▶

- Colour separation lines, see main views for colours.
- Tie-down eye.
- Oil drain pipe.
- Titanium spring blade undercarriage.
- At rest position.
- Maximum unloaded position.

Exported to several nations. the Z 50L has equipped many aerobatic teams including that of Hungary. (R G Moulton)
▼

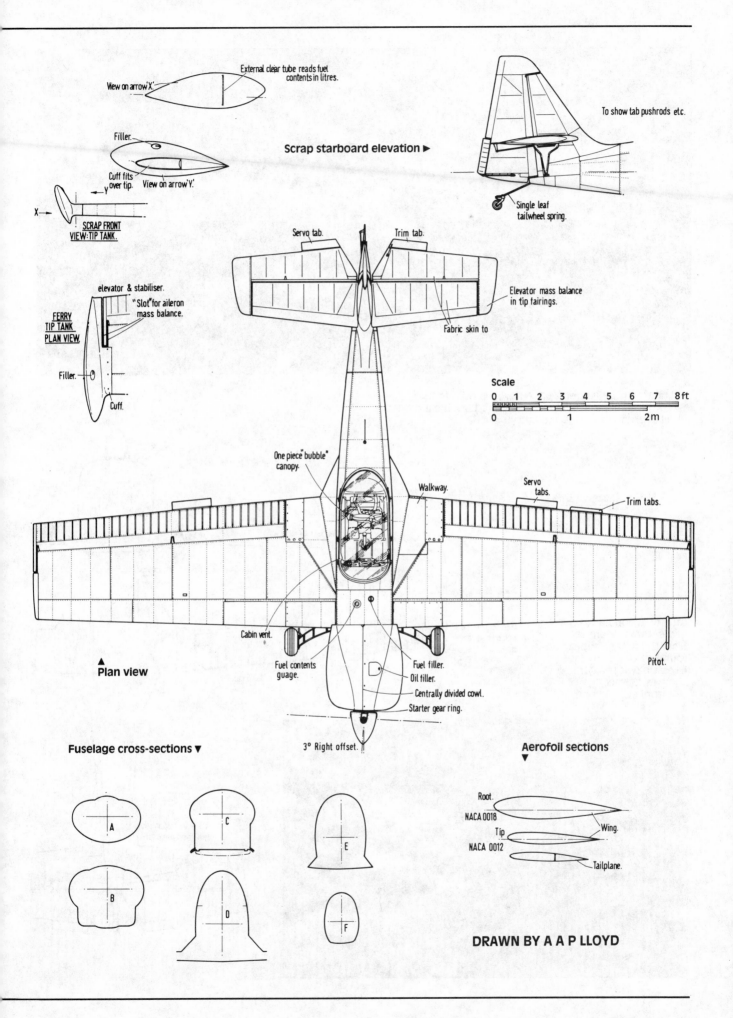

View on arrow 'X'.

External clear tube reads fuel contents in litres.

Scrap starboard elevation ▶

To show tab pushrods etc.

Filler.

Cuff fits over tip.

View on arrow 'Y'.

Single leaf tailwheel spring.

Y

X

SCRAP FRONT VIEW: TIP TANK.

Servo tab.

Trim tab.

elevator & stabiliser.

"Slot" for aileron mass balance.

FERRY TIP TANK PLAN VIEW.

Elevator mass balance in tip fairings.

Fabric skin to

Filler.

Cuff.

Scale

0 1 2 3 4 5 6 7 8 ft

0   1   2 m

One piece "bubble" canopy.

Walkway.

Servo tabs.

Trim tabs.

Cabin vent.

Fuel contents guage.

Fuel filler.

Oil filler.

Pitot.

Centrally divided cowl.

Starter gear ring.

▲ Plan view

3° Right offset.

Fuselage cross-sections ▼

Aerofoil sections ▼

A

B

C

D

E

F

Root.

NACA 0018

Wing.

Tip

NACA 0012

Tailplane.

DRAWN BY A A P LLOYD

▲
West German-registered Z 50L entered in the World
Aerobatic Championships. Introduced in 1975, the aircraft
is still in production. (D Boddington)

Scale

0 1 2 3 4 5 6 7 8 ft

0 1 2 m

Underplan
▼

3° Right thrust.

Drain.

One piece all metal wing.

Tie down eye.

Aileron mass balance.

Ailerons all metal
with external stiffen-
ing corrugations.

Servo tab.

Latest version has very
few external changes
from the first to appear
fourteen years previously.
As demo'd at the Paris Air
Show in 1989. (R G
Moulton)
▼

Stabiliser bracing struts
are hollow metal forms.

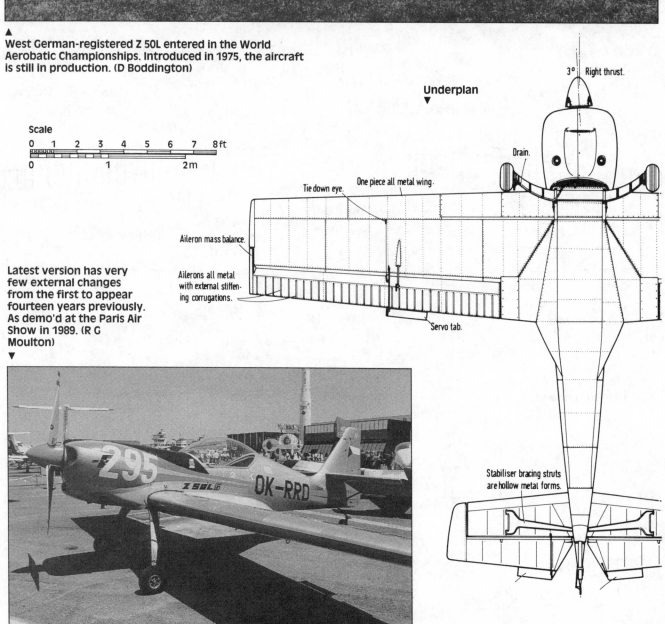

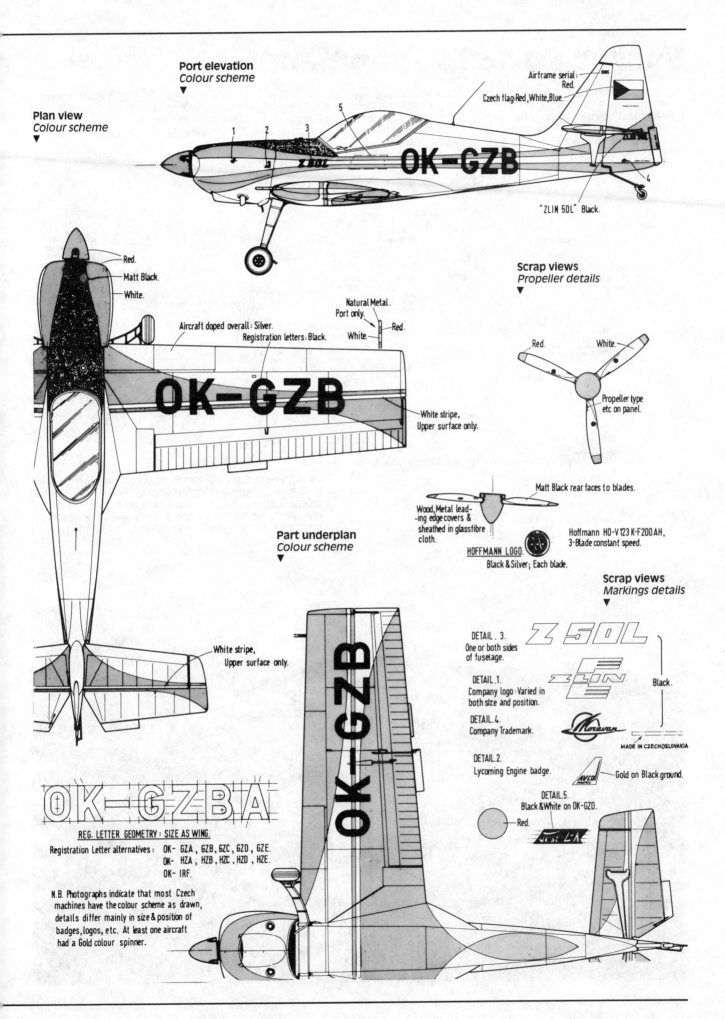

Plan view
Colour scheme
▼

Port elevation
Colour scheme
▼

Airframe serial:
Red.

Czech flag-Red, White, Blue.

OK-GZB

"ZLIN 50L" Black.

Red.

Matt Black.

White.

Natural Metal.
Port only.
Red.
White.

Aircraft doped overall: Silver.
Registration letters: Black.

OK-GZB

White stripe,
Upper surface only.

Scrap views
Propeller details
▼

Red.   White.

Propeller type
etc on panel.

Matt Black rear faces to blades.

Wood, Metal lead-
ing edge covers &
sheathed in glassfibre
cloth.

HOFFMANN LOGO.
Black & Silver; Each blade.

Hoffmann HO-V123 K-F200 AH,
3-Blade constant speed.

Part underplan
Colour scheme
▼

White stripe,
Upper surface only.

OK-GZB

Scrap views
Markings details
▼

DETAIL . 3.
One or both sides
of fuselage.

Z 50L

DETAIL .1.
Company logo: Varied in
both size and position.

ZLIN

Black.

DETAIL. 4.
Company Trademark.

Moravan

MADE IN CZECHOSLOVAKIA

DETAIL.2.
Lycoming Engine badge.

AVCO

Gold on Black ground.

DETAIL.5.
Black & White on OK-GZD.

Red.

OK-GZBA

REG. LETTER GEOMETRY: SIZE AS WING.

Registration Letter alternatives : OK- GZA , GZB , GZC , GZD , GZE.
OK- HZA , HZB , HZC , HZD , HZE.
OK- IRF.

N.B. Photographs indicate that most Czech
machines have the colour scheme as drawn,
details differ mainly in size & position of
badges, logos, etc. At least one aircraft
had a Gold colour spinner.

Bücker Bü 131B Jungmann

Country of origin: Germany.
Type: Two-seat aerobatic aircraft.
Powerplant: One Hirth HM504 air-cooled engine rated at 105hp or (Pilatus-modified aircraft) Lycoming IO-360 rated at 180hp.

Dimensions: Wing span 24ft 3in *7.40m*; length 21ft 8in *6.62m*; height 7ft 5in *2.25m*; wing area 145 sq ft *13.5m²*
Weights: Empty 838lb *380kg*; loaded 1477lb *670kg*.
Performance: Maximum speed 114mph

183.5kph; time to 6500ft *1980m*, 12min; service ceiling 14,100ft *4300m*; range 404 miles *650km*.
First flight: 27 April 1934.

Colour division.

Venturi, St'bd side.

BLACK. RED. GOLD. German ensign.

D.GREEN Chequered pattern.

Cowl, L.edges of wings & u/c fairings & undersides of lower wings fuselage & tail : D.GREEN.

Chess knight : BLACK.

D.GREEN. YELLOW.

Inspection zips.

Hand holds.

G-ATJX

Unloaded, flying position.

▲ Port elevation

DRAWN BY E A COATES AND A A P LLOYD

◀ **Scrap starboard elevation**
Cowling

Though a standard *Luftwaffe* trainer, it was the Swiss who brought the Jungmann to prominence in international aerobatics. HB-EKA is typical of this prized aristocrat. The other source is Spain, which released batches from Air Force duties to Britain and the USA.
▼

Bright yellow and black CASA (Spanish) version restored by Tony Smith was shipped to Darwin and flown back solo by Tony between 29 April and 22 May 1989. He quoted Neil Williams: 'Nothing flies like a Bücker'.

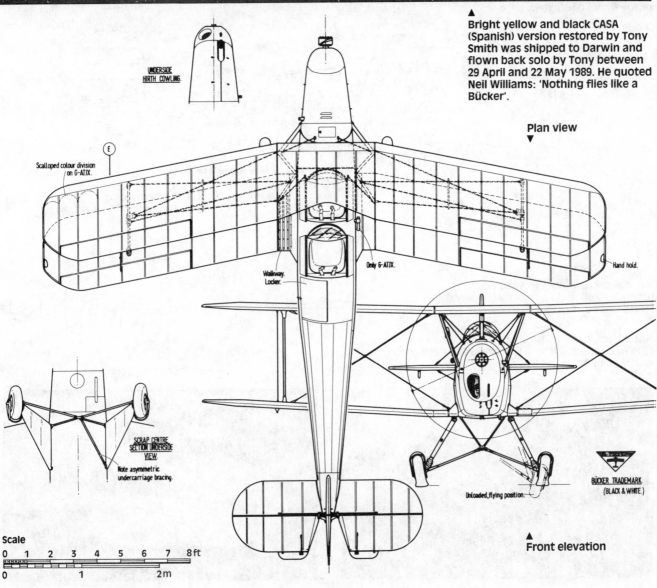

UNDERSIDE HIRTH COWLING.

Plan view
▼

Scalloped colour division on G-ATJX.

Only G-ATJX.

Walkway.
Locker.

Hand hold.

SCRAP CENTRE SECTION UNDERSIDE VIEW.

Note asymmetric undercarriage bracing.

Unloaded, flying position.

BÜCKER TRADEMARK.
(BLACK & WHITE.)

▲
Front elevation

Scale
0 1 2 3 4 5 6 7 8ft
0   1   2m

▲
After the original Hirth 504 engine on German and Swiss aircraft (as drawn), licence-built versions had a wide range of engines.

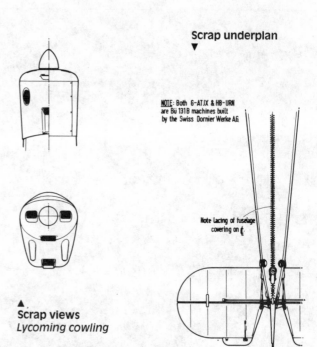

Scrap underplan
▼

NOTE: Both G-ATJX & HB-URN are Bü 131B machines built by the Swiss Dornier Werke A.G.

Note lacing of fuselage covering on ₵

▲ Scrap views
Lycoming cowling

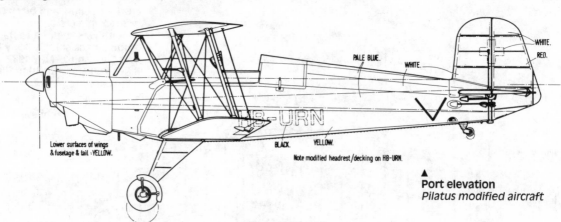

PALE BLUE.

WHITE.

WHITE.
RED.

Lower surfaces of wings & fuselage & tail : YELLOW.

BLACK. YELLOW.

Note modified headrest/decking on HB-URN.

▲ Port elevation
Pilatus modified aircraft

Narrow-chord wings are swept back 11° to give better cockpit access, making the centre-section struts quite distinctive.
▼

Wing section 'E'
▼

Slot-effect elevators protrude above or below tailplane on deflection, a feature of Bücker designs which gives powerful control.
▼ ▶

A   B   C   D

▲ Fuselage cross-sections

Wagner-Hirth Acrostar I and II

Country of origin: West Germany/Switzerland.
Type: Single-seat aerobatic aircraft
Powerplant: One Franklin 6A-350-CL engine rated at 220hp.

Dimensions: Wing span 27ft 2in *8.28m*; length 20ft 0in *6.11m*; height 5ft 10in *1.78m*.
Weights: Empty 1069lb *485kg*.
Performance: Maximum speed

192.5mph *310kph*; climb rate 2950ft/min *900m/min*; load limit +8/−8g.
First flight: 1970.

DRAWN BY A A P LLOYD

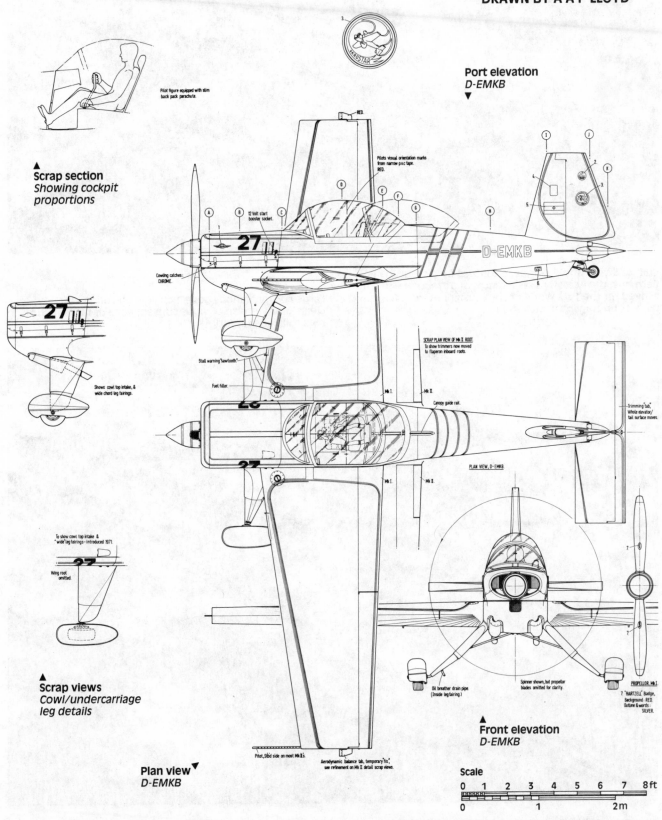

Scrap section
Showing cockpit proportions

Pilot figure equipped with slim back pack parachute.

Port elevation
D-EMKB
▼

RED.

Pilots visual orientation marks from narrow p.v.c tape. RED.

12 Volt start booster socket.

Cowling catches. CHROME.

D-EMKB

Stall warning 'sawtooth'.

Fuel filler.

Shows cowl top intake, & wide chord leg fairings.

SCRAP PLAN VIEW OF Mk II ROOT.
To show trimmers now moved to flaperon inboard roots.

Mk I.   Mk II.

Canopy guide rail.

Trimming 'tab', Whole elevator/tail surface moves.

PLAN VIEW, D-EMKB.

Mk I.   Mk II.

To show cowl top intake & "wide" leg fairings - introduced 1971.

Wing root omitted.

Scrap views
Cowl/undercarriage leg details

Pilot, Stbd side on most Mk II's.

Aerodynamic balance tab, temporary 'fix', see refinement on Mk II detail scrap views.

Plan view ▼
D-EMKB

Oil breather drain pipe. (Inside leg fairing.)

Spinner shown, but propellor blades omitted for clarity.

PROPELLOR, Mk I.

7. 'HARTZELL' Badge. Background : RED. Outline & words : SILVER.

Front elevation
D-EMKB

Scale

| 0 | 1 | 2 | 3 | 4 | 5 | 6 | 7 | 8ft |

| 0 | | 1 | | 2m |

▲
Built to Swiss Arnold Wagner's concept by Wolf Hirth in Germany, the Acrostar was a centre of attraction when it arrived for the 1970 World Championships at Hullavington with its unusual control system.

Large cockpit canopy gave excellent all-round visibility; clean lines were an obvious consequence of manufacture by a sailplane factory.
▼

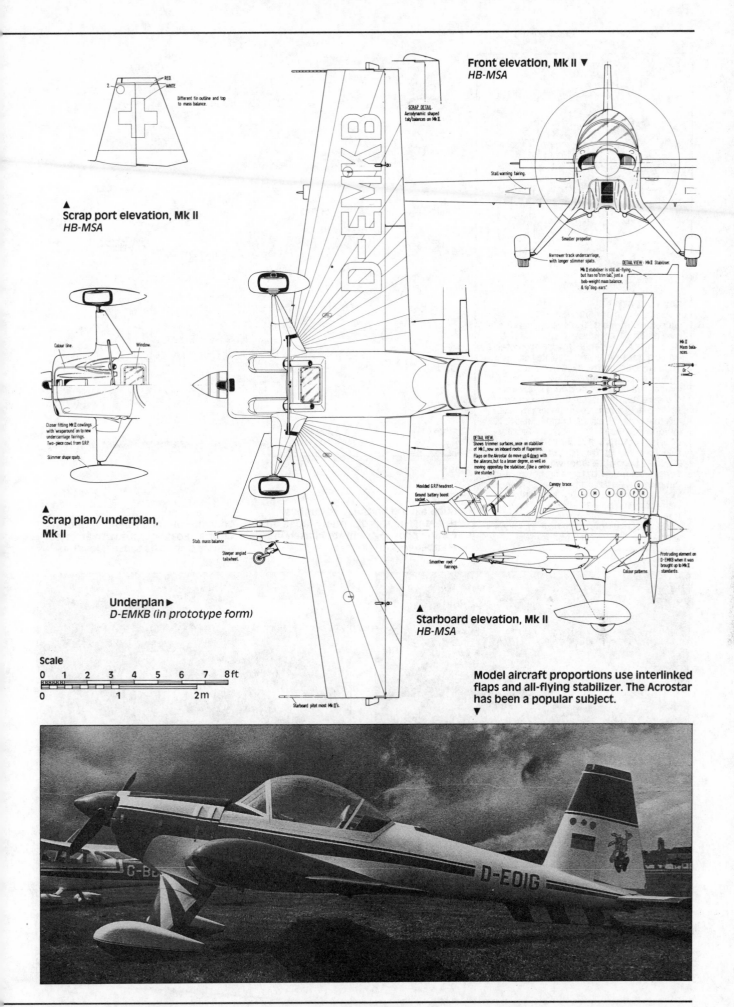

Scrap port elevation, Mk II
HB-MSA

2.
RED.
WHITE
Different fin outline and top to mass balance.

SCRAP DETAIL
Aerodynamic shaped tab/balances on Mk II.

Front elevation, Mk II ▼
HB-MSA

Stall warning fairing.

Smaller propellor.

Narrower track undercarriage, with longer slimmer spats.

DETAIL VIEW : Mk II Stabiliser.
Mk II stabiliser is still all-flying, but has no 'trim tab', just a bob-weight mass balance, & tip 'dog-ears'.

Mk II Mass balances.

Or

Colour line.

Window.

Closer fitting Mk II cowlings with 'wraparound' on to new undercarriage fairings.
Two-piece cowl from G.R.P.

Slimmer shape spats.

Scrap plan/underplan, Mk II

Stab. mass balance

Steeper angled tailwheel.

DETAIL VIEW.
Shows trimmer surfaces, once on stabiliser of Mk I, now on inboard roots of flaperons.
Flaps on the Acrostar do move up & down with the ailerons, but to a lesser degree, as well as moving oppositely the stabiliser. (like a control-line stunter.)

Moulded G.R.P.headrest.
Ground battery boost socket.

Canopy brace.

L   M   N   O   P   R   Q

Smoother root fairings.

Protruding element on D-EMKB when it was brought up to Mk II standards.

Colour patterns.

Underplan ▶
D-EMKB (in prototype form)

Starboard elevation, Mk II
HB-MSA

Starboard pilot most Mk II's.

Scale

0 1 2 3 4 5 6 7 8 ft

0   1   2m

Model aircraft proportions use interlinked flaps and all-flying stabilizer. The Acrostar has been a popular subject.
▼

D-EMKB

G-BE

D-EOIG

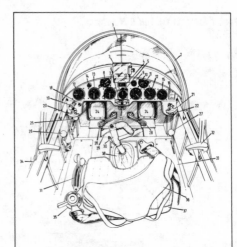

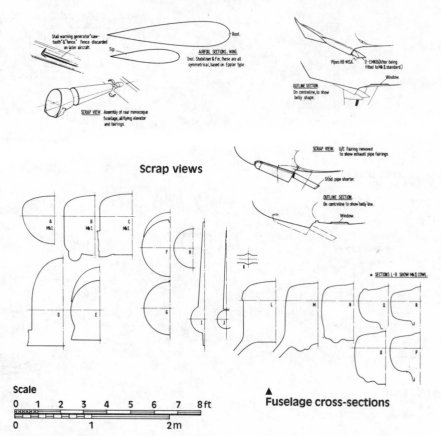

Scrap views

Scale

```
0   1   2   3   4   5   6   7   8 ft
0            1            2m
```

▲ **Fuselage cross-sections**

Key to cockpit
1. Pilot's alignment lines (tape). 2. Windshield frame. 3. Transparent sequence card holder. 4. Compass. 5. Stopwatch. 6. Slip ball. 7. Altimeter. 8. 'G' accelerometer. 9. Exhaust gas temperature. 10. Rev counter. 11. 'G' accelerometer. 12. Combined temperature/pressure gauge. 13. Airspeed indicator. 14. Starter button. 15. Manifold pressure. 16. Limit card. 17. Climb/descent. 18. Smoke ignition. 19. Propeller pitch. 20. Alternate engine air. 21. Engine cut-off. 22. Ignition and magneto switch. 23. Battery booster socket. 24. Rudder pedals. 25. Fuel selector lever. 26. Throttle. 27. Fuel pump. 28. Brake pedals. 29. Floor window panel. 30. Control column with transmit button and Din plug. 31. Flaps and trimmer. 32. Canopy lock handles (in locked position aft). 33. Mainspar wing box. 34. Sliding canopy frame. 35. Harness centre lock boss. 36. Abdominal pad (for aerobatics). 37. Pilot's seat squab. 38. Canvas 'boot' for stick.

Bubble hood on the Acrostar has reference marks discreetly taped on for the pilot to orientate himself in manoeuvres. (P Lloyd)
▼

Control column is reminiscent of WWI German Fokker types with an offset handle grip at its top. (P Lloyd)
▼

Colour notes
Underside of D-EMKB shows orange/beige 'sunburst' pattern with registration letters in black. This scheme had its basic colours altered with the new cowl update in 1972. HB-MSA indicated here was finished white overall; anti-dazzle cowl top – black; spinner – red striped white; fuselage 'speedbird' stripe, fin, wing/tailplane tip bands and leading-edge stripes, half-spats, underfin bands and fuselage spine stripe – red. Registration letters on fuselage and under wing – black.

Views of D-EMKB show the prototype

Acrostar Mk I as inspected at the 1970 World Aerobatic Championships. The finish and intricacies of the colour scheme can best be followed from the photographs. The following were the colours: Overall finish – cream; fuselage bands, accent areas, flying surface edges and roots, underwing sunburst etc – orange/beige; competition number, registration and trim stripes – black; cockpit interior structure – light grey; propeller – pale grey with yellow tips; rear faces and cowl anti-dazzle patch – matt black. Badge details are as follows: 1.

'Franklin' in script and wings – silver; oval base ground – red; detail – black. 2. 'Wolf Hirth – Nabern' – black; disc – mid-blue; bird silhouette – white. 3. Aircraft – yellow; helmet and details – red; 'contrails' – blue; outer circle – orange; 'Acrostar' – white. 4. 'W/Champs Hullavington' – red, blue on white. 5. Federal German ensign – top bar black, then red and gold. This indicated the origin of the aircraft and one of its pilots; the other pilot was Swiss, so a tiny white cross made the centre bar a Swiss flag. 6. Manufacturer's plate – brass.

Bede BD-8

Country of origin: USA.
Type: Single-seat aerobatic aircraft.
Powerplant: One Lycoming engine rated at 200hp.
Dimensions: Wing span 19ft 4in *5.89m*; length 17ft 0in *5.18m*; height 6ft 9in *2.06m*.
Weights: Empty 700lb *317kg*; loaded 900lb *408kg*.
Performance: Maximum speed over 185mph *300kph* at 500ft *150m*; climb rate over 2000ft/min *610m/min*; stalling speed 65mph *105kph*; roll rate 190°/sec.
First flight: 1979.

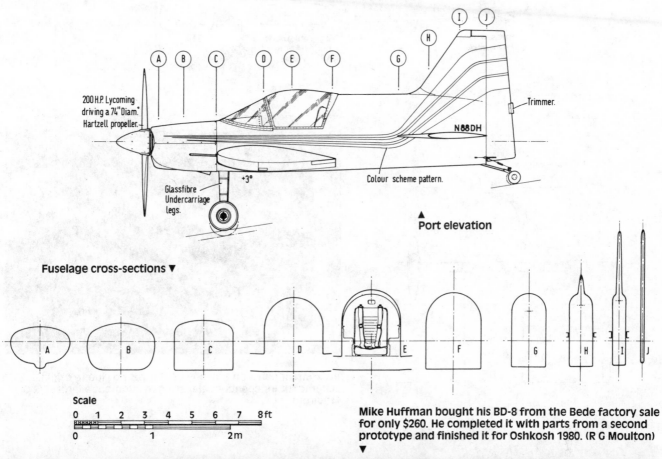

200 H.P. Lycoming driving a 74" Diam. Hartzell propeller.

Glassfibre Undercarriage legs.

+3°

Trimmer.

N88DH

Colour scheme pattern.

▲ Port elevation

Fuselage cross-sections ▼

A   B   C   D   E   F   G   H   I   J

Scale

0 1 2 3 4 5 6 7 8ft

0   1   2m

Mike Huffman bought his BD-8 from the Bede factory sale for only $260. He completed it with parts from a second prototype and finished it for Oshkosh 1980. (R G Moulton)
▼

N88DH

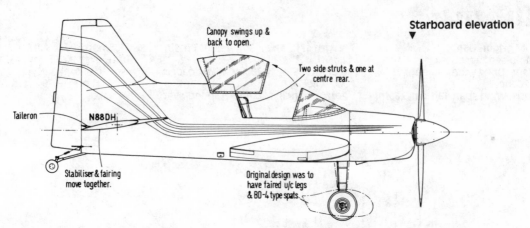

Starboard elevation ▼

Canopy swings up & back to open.

Two side struts & one at centre rear.

Taileron

N88DH

Stabiliser & fairing move together.

Original design was to have faired u/c legs & BD-4 type spats.

Scrap underplan ▼

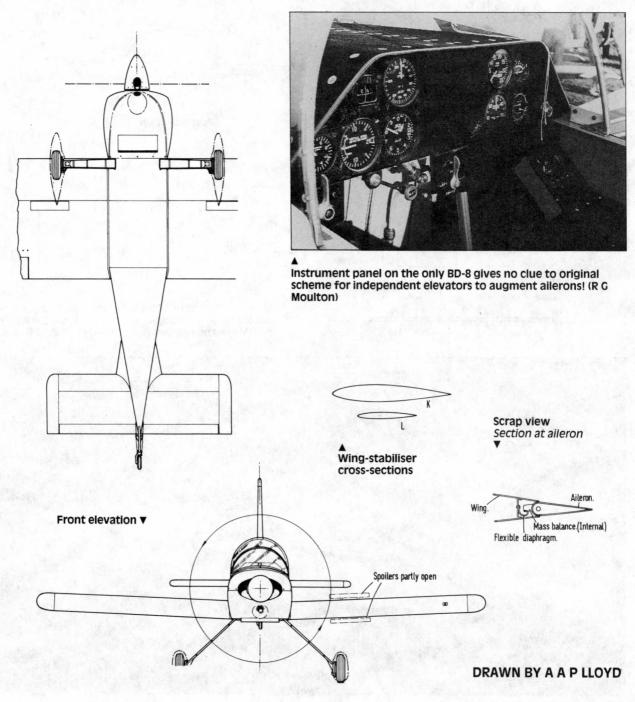

▲ Instrument panel on the only BD-8 gives no clue to original scheme for independent elevators to augment ailerons! (R G Moulton)

K

L

▲ Wing-stabiliser cross-sections

Scrap view
Section at aileron
▼

Wing.

Aileron.

Mass balance. (Internal)

Flexible diaphragm.

Front elevation ▼

Spoilers partly open

DRAWN BY A A P LLOYD

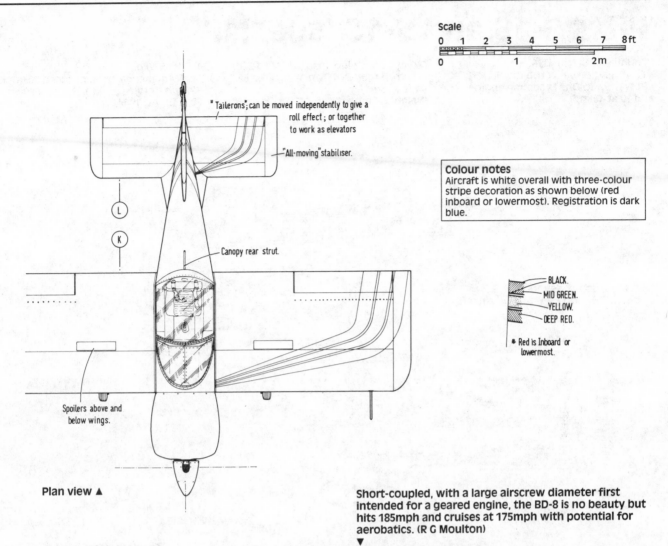

Scale

0 1 2 3 4 5 6 7 8 ft

0 1 2m

"Tailerons", can be moved independently to give a roll effect; or together to work as elevators

"All-moving" stabiliser.

Colour notes
Aircraft is white overall with three-colour stripe decoration as shown below (red inboard or lowermost). Registration is dark blue.

Canopy rear strut.

BLACK.
MID GREEN.
YELLOW.
DEEP RED.

* Red is inboard or lowermost.

Spoilers above and below wings.

Plan view ▲

Short-coupled, with a large airscrew diameter first intended for a geared engine, the BD-8 is no beauty but hits 185mph and cruises at 175mph with potential for aerobatics. (R G Moulton)
▼

Pitts S-1S and S-1C 'Special'

Country of origin: USA.
Type: Single-seat aerobatic aircraft.
Powerplant: One Lycoming engine rated at 180hp.

Dimensions: Wing span 17ft 4in *5.28m*; length 15ft 5½in *4.71m*; wing area 98.5 sq ft *9.15m²*.
Weights: Empty 720lb *327kg*; maximum

1150lb *522kg*.
Performance: Maximum speed 203mph *327kph*; service ceiling 22,300ft *6800m*.
First flight: 1944.

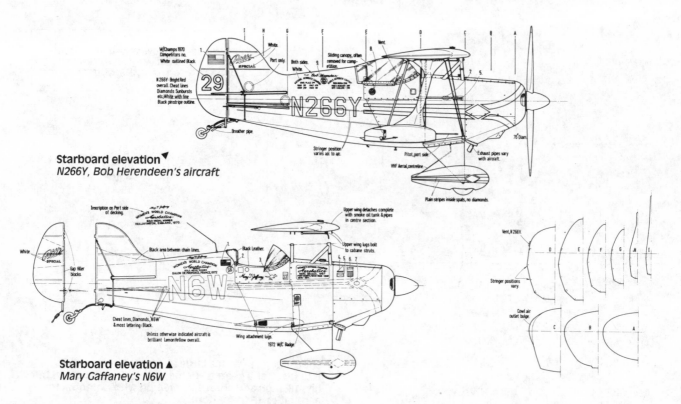

Starboard elevation ▼
N266Y, Bob Herendeen's aircraft

Starboard elevation ▲
Mary Gaffaney's N6W

▲
Fuselage cross-sections

German entry at the World Championships 1986 at South Cerny, the ever-young S-1S was by then a 46-year-old design. (D Boddington)
▼

▲ Transparent fuselage panels provide downward (or upward!) vision as on this modified S-1S at the 1986 World Championships from Sweden. (D Boddington)

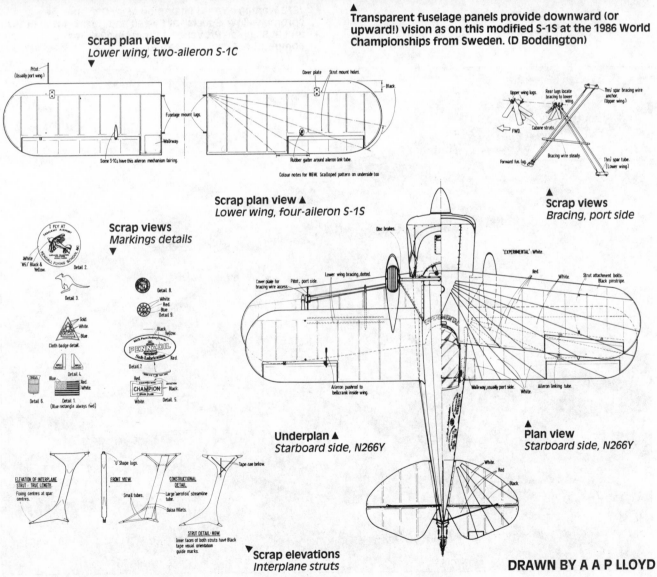

Scrap plan view
Lower wing, two-aileron S-1C
▼

Scrap plan view ▲
Lower wing, four-aileron S-1S

▲ **Scrap views**
Bracing, port side

Scrap views
Markings details
▼

Underplan ▲
Starboard side, N266Y

▲ **Plan view**
Starboard side, N266Y

▼**Scrap elevations**
Interplane struts

DRAWN BY A A P LLOYD

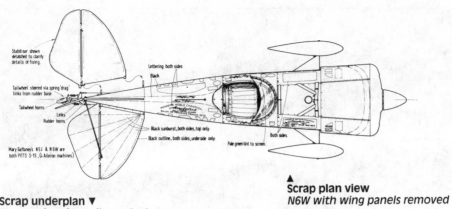

Stabiliser shown detached to clarify details of fixing.

Lettering both sides

Black

Tailwheel steered via spring 'drag' links from rudder base.

Tailwheel horns.

Links.

Rudder horns.

Mary Gaffaney's N5J & N6W are both PITTS S-1S, (4 Aileron machines.)

Black sunburst, both sides, top only.

Black outline, both sides, underside only.

Pale green tint to screen.

Both sides.

Scrap plan view
N6W with wing panels removed

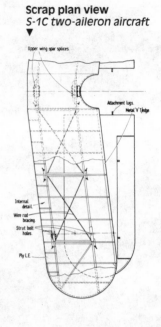

Scrap plan view
S-1C two-aileron aircraft
▼

Upper wing spar splices.

Attachment lugs.

Metal 'V' ledge.

Internal detail.

Wire rod bracing.

Strut bolt holes.

Ply L.E.

Scrap underplan ▼
Upper wing, four-aileron S-1S

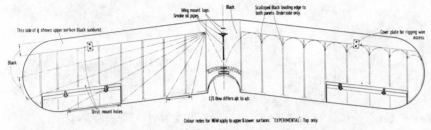

This side of ₵ shows upper surface Black sunburst.

Black

Wing mount lugs.
Smoke oil pipes.

Black

Scalloped Black leading edge to both panels. Underside only.

Cover plate for rigging wire access.

Strut mount holes.

C/S Bow differs a/c to a/c.

Colour notes for N6W apply to upper & lower surfaces. 'EXPERIMENTAL': Top only.

Scale

1972 Women's World Champion Mary Gaffeney flew this chrome yellow 'Special' at Sywell and Hullavington in 1970 and at Salon de Provence, France, in 1972. It would still be competitive today. (R G Moulton)
▼

One of three all-red Pitts S-1s flown by the 1970 US Team of Gene Soucy, Bob Herendeen and Charlie Hilliard. With a 200hp engine and constant-speed propeller they were called S-1T versions.

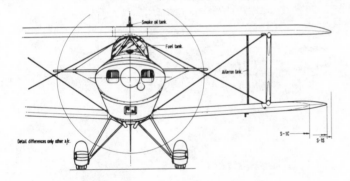

Front elevation
N266Y

Wing and tailplane sections ▶

TYPICAL TAIL SURFACE SECTION

CENTRE-SECTION

TYPICAL S-1S.

TYPICAL S-1C.

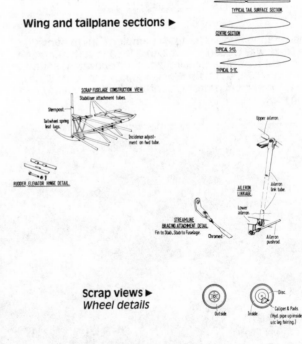

Scrap views ▶
Wheel details

◀ The tight cockpit of the S-1 offers little room for radio aids and is specifically aimed at short-range VFR flights between aerobatics. (R G Moulton)

Sukhoi Su-26M

Country of origin: USSR.
Type: Single-seat aerobatic aircraft.
Powerplant: One M-14P engine rated at 360hp.

Dimensions: Wing span 25ft 7in *7.80m*; length 22ft 5in *6.82m*.
Weights: Empty 1775lb *805kg*.
Performance: Maximum speed 205mph

330kph; load limit +12/−10g.
First flight: 1984.

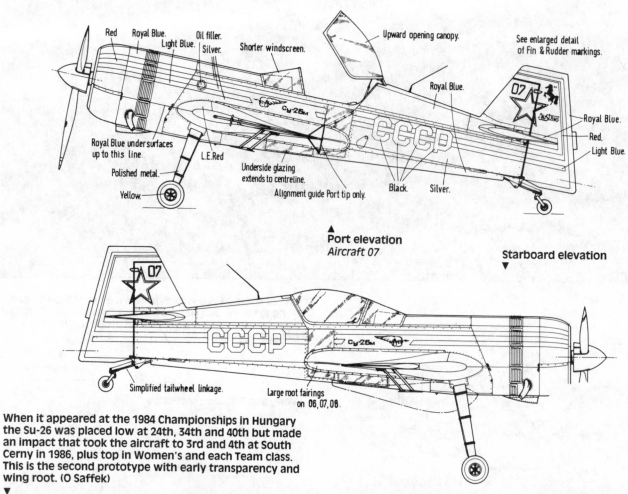

Red — Royal Blue. — Light Blue. — Oil filler. — Silver. — Shorter windscreen. — Upward opening canopy. — See enlarged detail of Fin & Rudder markings.

Royal Blue.

Royal Blue under surfaces up to this line.

Polished metal.

Yellow.

L.E.Red.

Underside glazing extends to centreline.

Alignment guide Port tip only.

Black. — Silver.

Royal Blue. — Red. — Light Blue.

07

▲ **Port elevation**
Aircraft 07

Starboard elevation ▼

07

Simplified tailwheel linkage.

Large root fairings on 06, 07, 08.

When it appeared at the 1984 Championships in Hungary the Su-26 was placed low at 24th, 34th and 40th but made an impact that took the aircraft to 3rd and 4th at South Cerny in 1986, plus top in Women's and each Team class. This is the second prototype with early transparency and wing root. (O Saffek)
▼

▲
For 1986, the Su-26 had wing root fairings. This is 07, with a simplified tailwheel linkage and sundry detail changes. (R G Moulton)

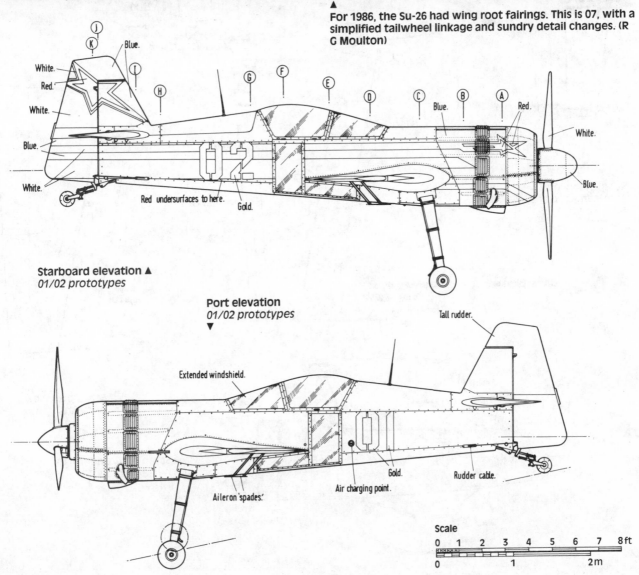

J
K
Blue.
White.
Red.
White.
Blue.
White.
Red undersurfaces to here.
Gold.
H
G
F
E
D
C
B
A
Blue.
Red.
White.
Blue.

Starboard elevation ▲
01/02 prototypes

Port elevation
01/02 prototypes
▼

Tall rudder.
Extended windshield.
Aileron 'spades'.
Air charging point.
Gold.
Rudder cable.

Scale
0 1 2 3 4 5 6 7 8 ft
0   1   2m

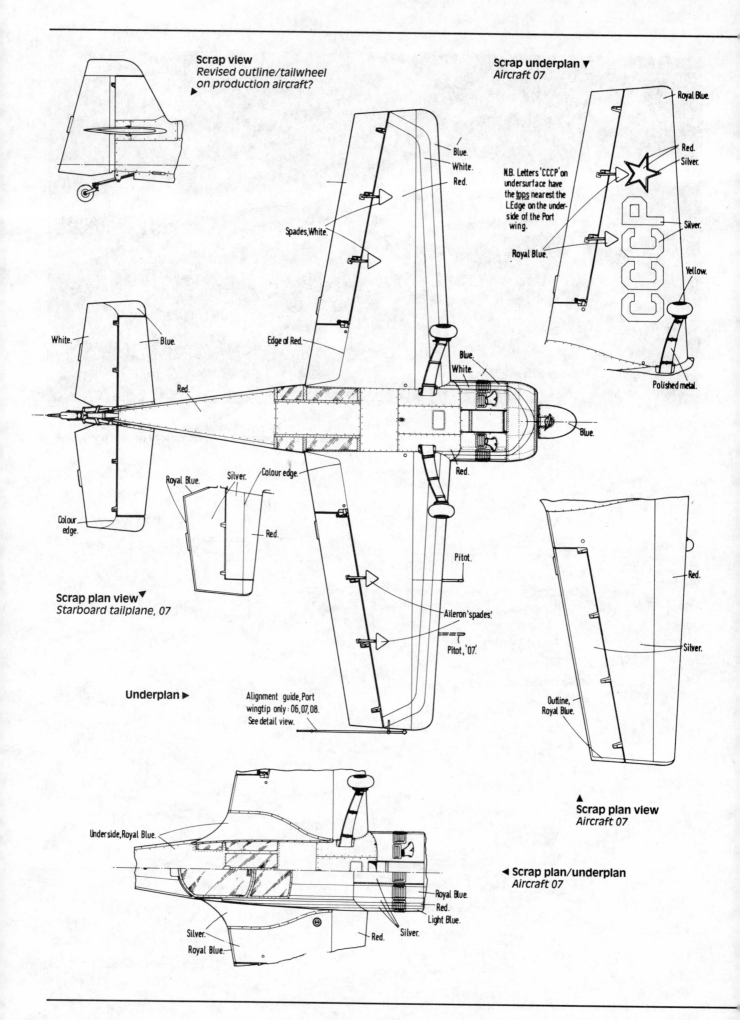

Scrap view
Revised outline/tailwheel
on production aircraft?
▶

Scrap underplan ▼
Aircraft 07

Royal Blue.

Blue.
White.
Red.

N.B. Letters 'CCCP' on
undersurface have
the <u>tops</u> nearest the
L.Edge on the under-
side of the Port
wing.

Red.
Silver.

Spades, White.

Royal Blue.

Silver.

White.

Blue.

Yellow.

Edge of Red.

Blue.
White.

Red.

Polished metal.

Red.

Blue.

Royal Blue.

Silver.

Colour edge.

Red.

Colour
edge.

Red.

Pitot.

Scrap plan view ▼
Starboard tailplane, 07

Aileron 'spades'.

Pitot, '07'.

Silver.

Underplan ▶

Alignment guide, Port
wingtip only: 06, 07, 08.
See detail view.

Outline,
Royal Blue.

▲
Scrap plan view
Aircraft 07

◀ **Scrap plan/underplan**
Aircraft 07

Underside, Royal Blue.

Royal Blue.
Red.
Light Blue.

Silver.

Silver.

Red.

Royal Blue.

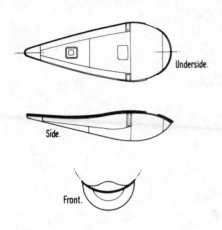

Underside.

Side.

Front.

Scrap views ▲
Auxiliary fuel tank

▲
Titanium undercarriage has considerable deflection off-load – see drawings. The propeller is a Hoffman unit bought from West Germany. (P Lloyd)

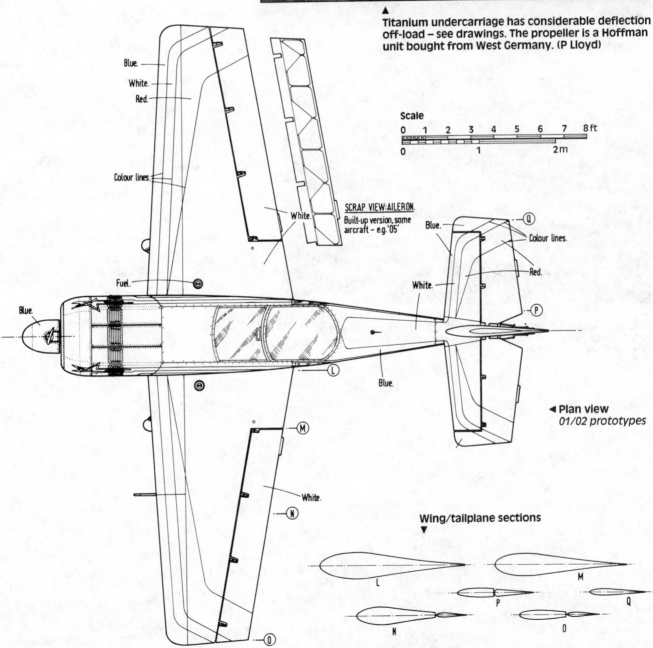

Blue.

White.

Red.

Colour lines.

White.

SCRAP VIEW: AILERON.
Built-up version, some
aircraft – e.g. '05'

Fuel.

Blue.

Blue.

White.

Blue.

Colour lines.

Red.

White.

L

M

White.

N

O

Q

P

Scale

0 1 2 3 4 5 6 7 8 ft

0   1   2m

◄ **Plan view**
01/02 prototypes

Wing/tailplane sections
▼

L

M

P

Q

N

O

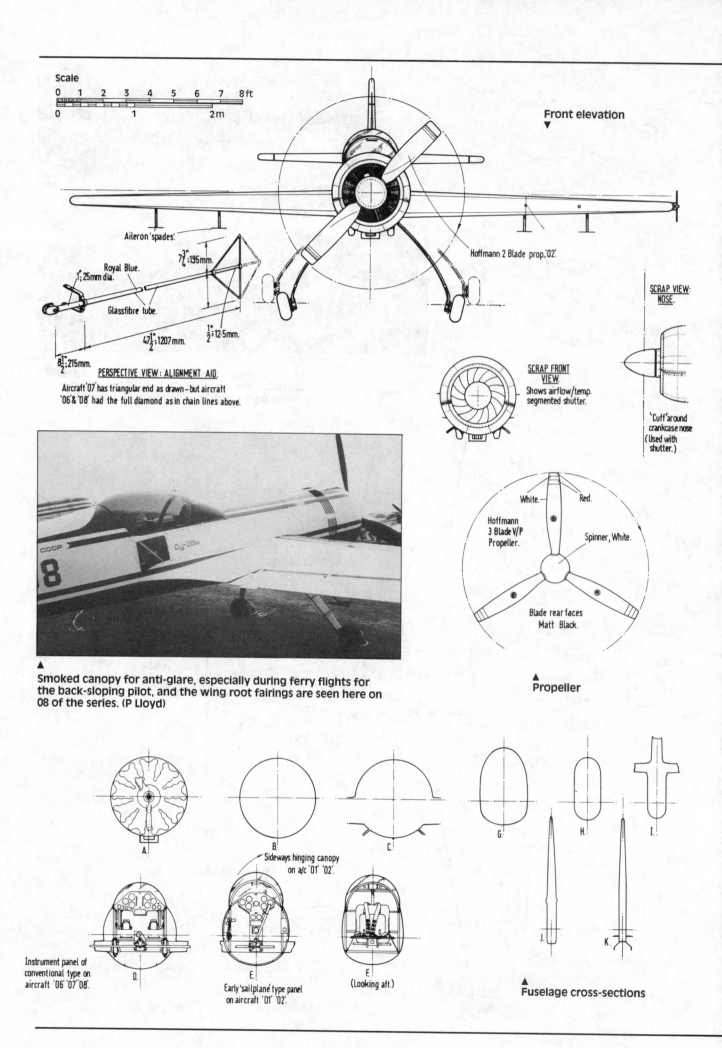

Scale

0 1 2 3 4 5 6 7 8 ft
0 1 2m

Front elevation
▼

Aileron 'spades'.

Royal Blue.

7 3/4"; 195mm.

1"; 25mm dia.

Glassfibre tube.

1/2"; 12·5mm.

47 1/2"; 1207mm.

8 1/2"; 215mm.

PERSPECTIVE VIEW: ALIGNMENT AID.

Aircraft '07' has triangular end as drawn – but aircraft '06' & '08' had the full diamond as in chain lines above.

Hoffmann 2 Blade prop.'02'.

SCRAP FRONT VIEW.
Shows airflow/temp. segmented shutter.

SCRAP VIEW: NOSE.

'Cuff' around crankcase nose (Used with shutter.)

White. — Red.

Hoffmann 3 Blade V/P Propeller.

Spinner, White.

Blade rear faces Matt Black.

▲
Propeller

Smoked canopy for anti-glare, especially during ferry flights for the back-sloping pilot, and the wing root fairings are seen here on 08 of the series. (P Lloyd)

A.

B.

Sideways hinging canopy on a/c '01' '02'.

C.

G.

H.

I.

Instrument panel of conventional type on aircraft '06' '07' '08'.

D.

E.

Early 'sailplane' type panel on aircraft '01' '02'.

F.
(Looking aft.)

J.

K.

▲
Fuselage cross-sections

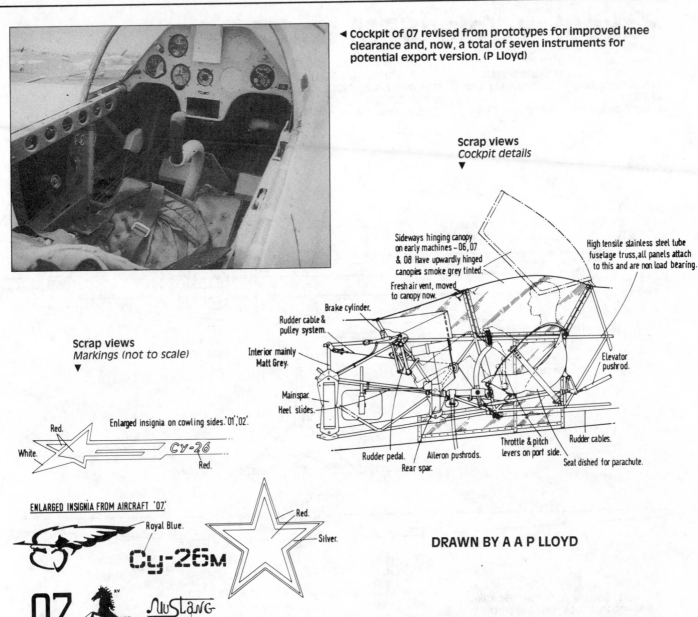

◄ Cockpit of 07 revised from prototypes for improved knee clearance and, now, a total of seven instruments for potential export version. (P Lloyd)

Scrap views
Cockpit details
▼

Sideways hinging canopy on early machines – 06, 07 & 08 Have upwardly hinged canopies smoke grey tinted.

Fresh air vent, moved to canopy now.

High tensile stainless steel tube fuselage truss, all panels attach to this and are non load bearing.

Brake cylinder.

Rudder cable & pulley system.

Interior mainly Matt Grey.

Elevator pushrod.

Mainspar.

Heel slides.

Rudder pedal.

Aileron pushrods.

Rear spar.

Throttle & pitch levers on port side.

Rudder cables.

Seat dished for parachute.

Scrap views
Markings (not to scale)
▼

Red.

White.

Cy-26

Red.

Enlarged insignia on cowling sides. '01','02'.

ENLARGED INSIGNIA FROM AIRCRAFT '07'.

Royal Blue.

Cy-26м

07

Black.

xv

Mustang

Royal Blue.

'S' Red.

Red.

Silver.

DRAWN BY A A P LLOYD

At the 1989 Paris Air Show, 04 appeared in purple and white with an altered cowling having extra louvres, and a new wing structure. (R G Moulton)
▼

Yakovlev Yak-18PM and PS

Country of origin: USSR.
Type: Single-seat aerobatic aircraft.
Powerplant: One AI-14FR engine rated at 300hp.
Dimensions: Wing span 34ft 9in *10.6m*; length 27ft 5in *8.35m*; height 11ft 0in *3.35m*, (PS) 9ft 7in *2.93m*.
Weights: Empty 1804lb *818kg*, (PS) 1819lb *825kg*.
Performance: Maximum speed 171mph 275kph, (PS) 200mph *320kph*; climb rate 1700ft/min *520m/min*, (PS) 2360ft/min *720m/min*; load limit +9/−6g.
First flight: 1966.

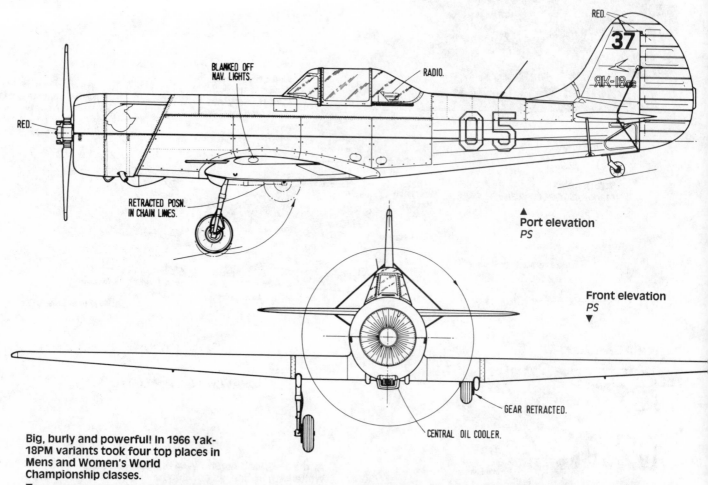

RED.

BLANKED OFF NAV. LIGHTS.

RADIO.

37

ЯК-18пс

RED.

05

RETRACTED POSN. IN CHAIN LINES.

Port elevation
PS

Front elevation
PS

GEAR RETRACTED.

CENTRAL OIL COOLER.

Big, burly and powerful! In 1966 Yak-18PM variants took four top places in Mens and Women's World Championship classes.

ЯК-18

ЯК-18

▲
Developed from the tricycle gear to taildragger for the PS
version, 05 and 08 at Hullavington in 1970. The Yak-50
development perpetuated its successes in 1976, 1978 and
1982. (R G Moulton)

Port elevation
PM
▼

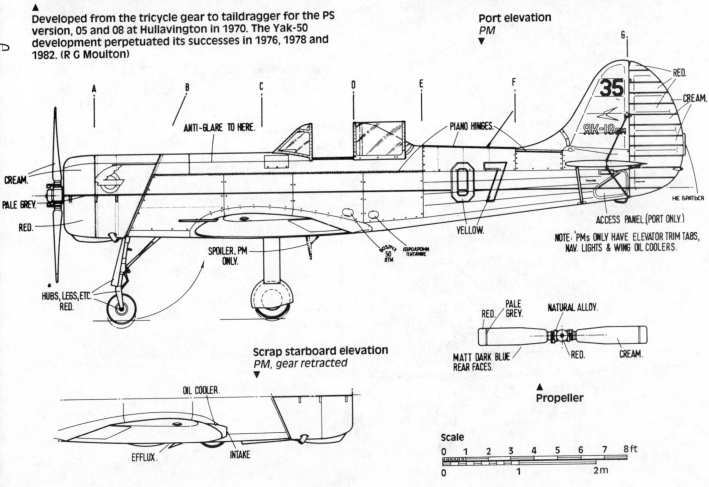

A B C D E F

ANTI-GLARE TO HERE.

PIANO HINGES.

6.

35

ЯК-18ПМ

RED.

CREAM.

CREAM.

PALE GREY.

RED.

07

SPOILER, PM
ONLY.

HUBS, LEGS, ETC.
RED.

YELLOW.

ВОЗДУХ
50
АТМ

АЭРОДРОМИ
ПИТАНИЕ

НЕ БРАТЬСЯ.

ACCESS PANEL (PORT ONLY.)

NOTE: PMs ONLY HAVE ELEVATOR TRIM TABS,
NAV. LIGHTS & WING OIL COOLERS.

Scrap starboard elevation
PM, gear retracted
▼

OIL COOLER.

EFFLUX.

INTAKE

RED.

PALE
GREY.

NATURAL ALLOY.

MATT DARK BLUE
REAR FACES.

RED.

CREAM.

▲
Propeller

Scale

0 1 2 3 4 5 6 7 8 ft

0   1   2 m

Colour notes

Fuselage – red below pale grey centreline stripe, cream above; matt dark blue anti-glare panel. Wing – cream with grey-outlined red trim on leading edge and tips; undersides red. Fin – cream. Rudder – cream and red stripes. Stabiliser – as wing. Fuselage codes – yellow with pale grey outline stripe. Trim tab note wording – red. Other access panel wording – black. Fin speedbird pale blue, type designation red with pale grey outline. Competition numbers – black. Wing undersides have yellow-outlined red star. Pitots are red and cream striped.

DRAWN BY A A P LLOYD

Scrap views
Insignia
▼

ENLARGED LAYOUT OF FIN LETTERING.

RED.   PALE GREY.

ЯК-1

WHITE.
GOLD.
BLACK.
DARK BLUE.
CCCP
ЦАК
☆
RED.
BLACK.
ИМ ЧКАЛОВА
PALE BLUE.

ENLARGED CENTRAL AERO CLUB BADGE. (ON COWL.)

NOTE: 'WING' FACES FORWARD BOTH SIDES OF COWL.

▲
Yak-18PM cockpit is equipped as for a trainer, with duplicated artiicial horizons and several G-meters.

Scrap underplan ▼
PS, port side

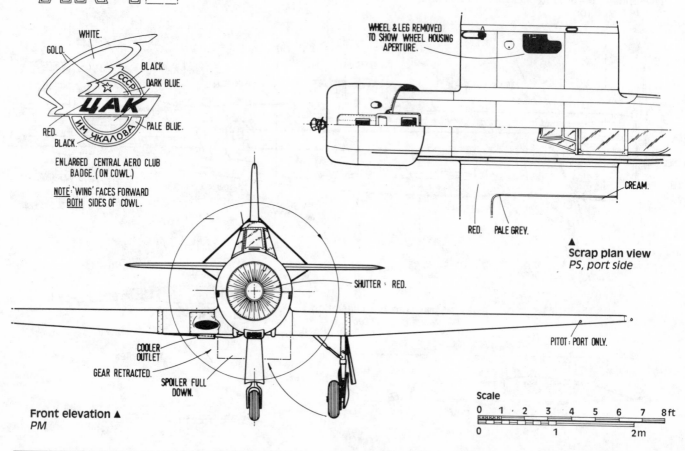

WHEEL & LEG REMOVED TO SHOW WHEEL HOUSING APERTURE.

CREAM.

RED.   PALE GREY.

▲
Scrap plan view
PS, port side

SHUTTER : RED.

PITOT : PORT ONLY.

COOLER OUTLET
GEAR RETRACTED.
SPOILER FULL DOWN.

Front elevation ▲
PM

Scale

0 1 2 3 4 5 6 7 8 ft

0   1   2m

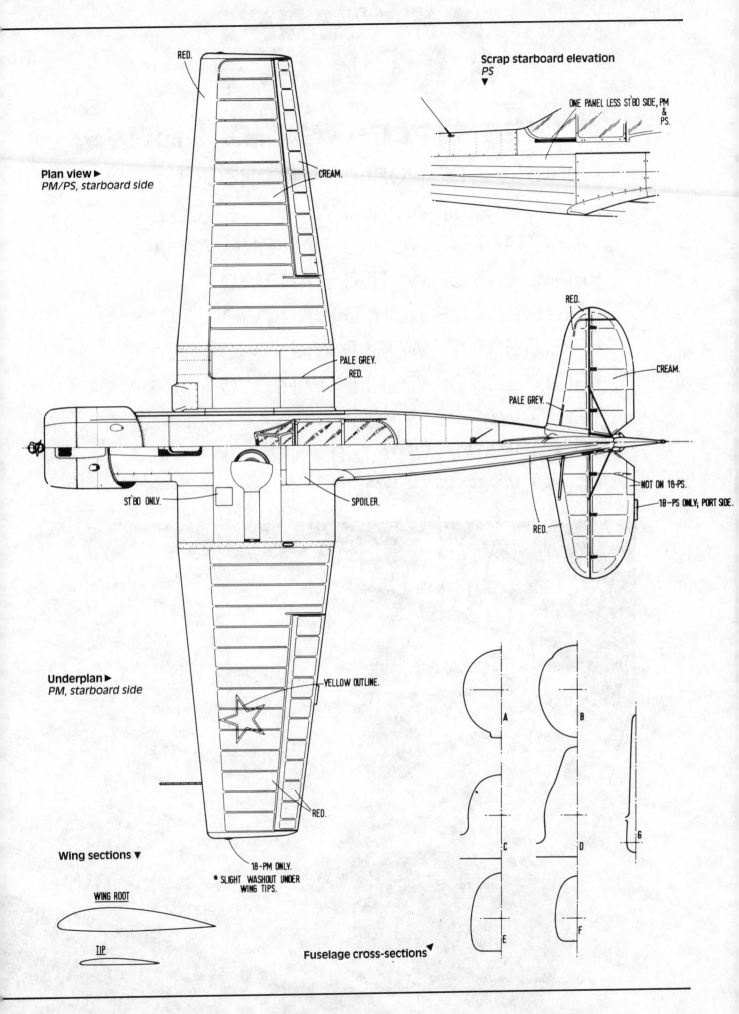

Plan view ▶
PM/PS, starboard side

RED.

CREAM.

Scrap starboard elevation
PS
▼

ONE PANEL LESS ST'BD SIDE, PM
&
PS.

PALE GREY.
RED.

RED.

CREAM.

PALE GREY.

NOT ON 18-PS.

18-PS ONLY; PORT SIDE.

RED.

ST'BO ONLY.

SPOILER.

Underplan ▶
PM, starboard side

YELLOW OUTLINE.

RED.

Wing sections ▼

WING ROOT

TIP

18-PM ONLY.
* SLIGHT WASHOUT UNDER
WING TIPS.

Fuselage cross-sections ◥

A

B

C

D

G

E

F